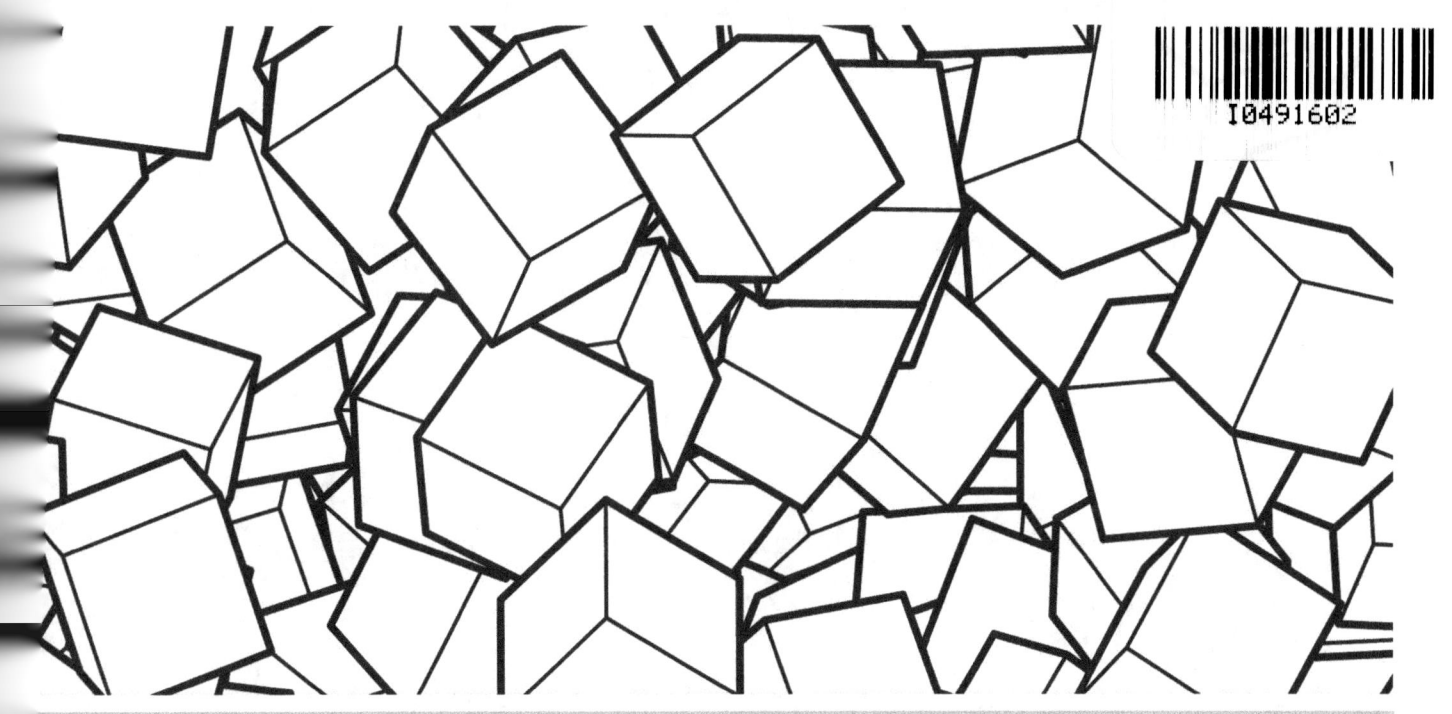

This book is given with love to my dad

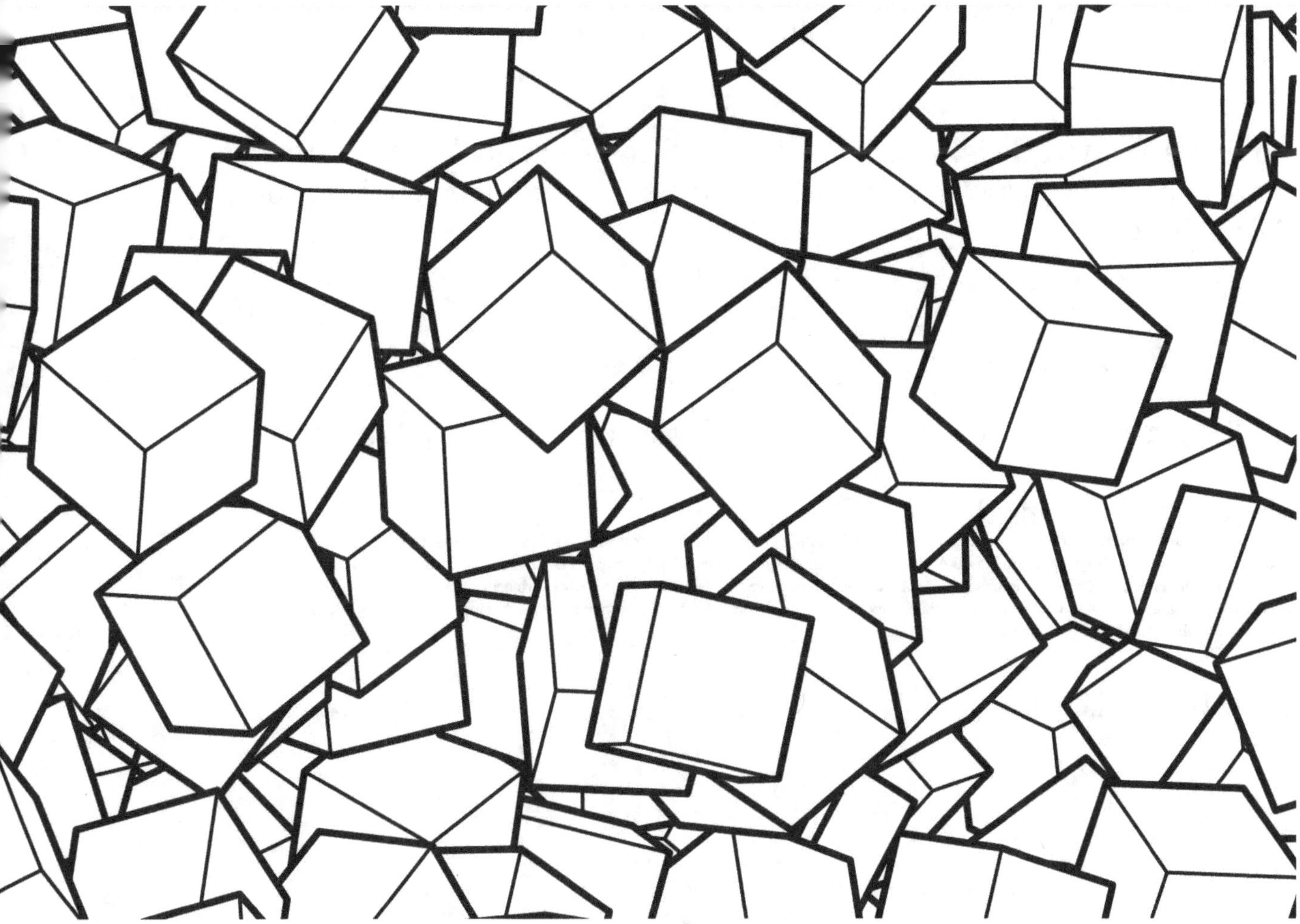

Love You Dad
The perfect anti-stress colouring book for fathers

First published in the United Kingdom in 2015 by
Bell & Mackenzie Publishing Limited

ISBN: 978-1-910771-40-2

A CIP catalogue record of this book is available from the British Library

Created by Christina Rose
Contributors: shutterstock/Nicemonkey, shutterstock/JOAT, shutterstock/Davor Ratkovic, shutterstock/Goldenarts, shutterstock/bekulnis, shutterstock/Polina Katritch, shutterstock/MastakA, shutterstock/Digital Saint, shutterstock/Nattaly, shutterstock/Olan, shutterstock/Marina Mandarina, shutterstock/Exclusivelly, shutterstock/Alex Landa, shutterstock/vector illustration, shutterstock/Trinochka, shutterstock/troyka, shutterstock/Regina Jershova, shutterstock/A-R-T, shutterstock/zubarevid, shutterstock/Bambuh, shutterstock/anfisa focusova, shutterstock/Lole, shutterstock/zubarevid, shutterstock/inraam

www.bellmackenzie.com

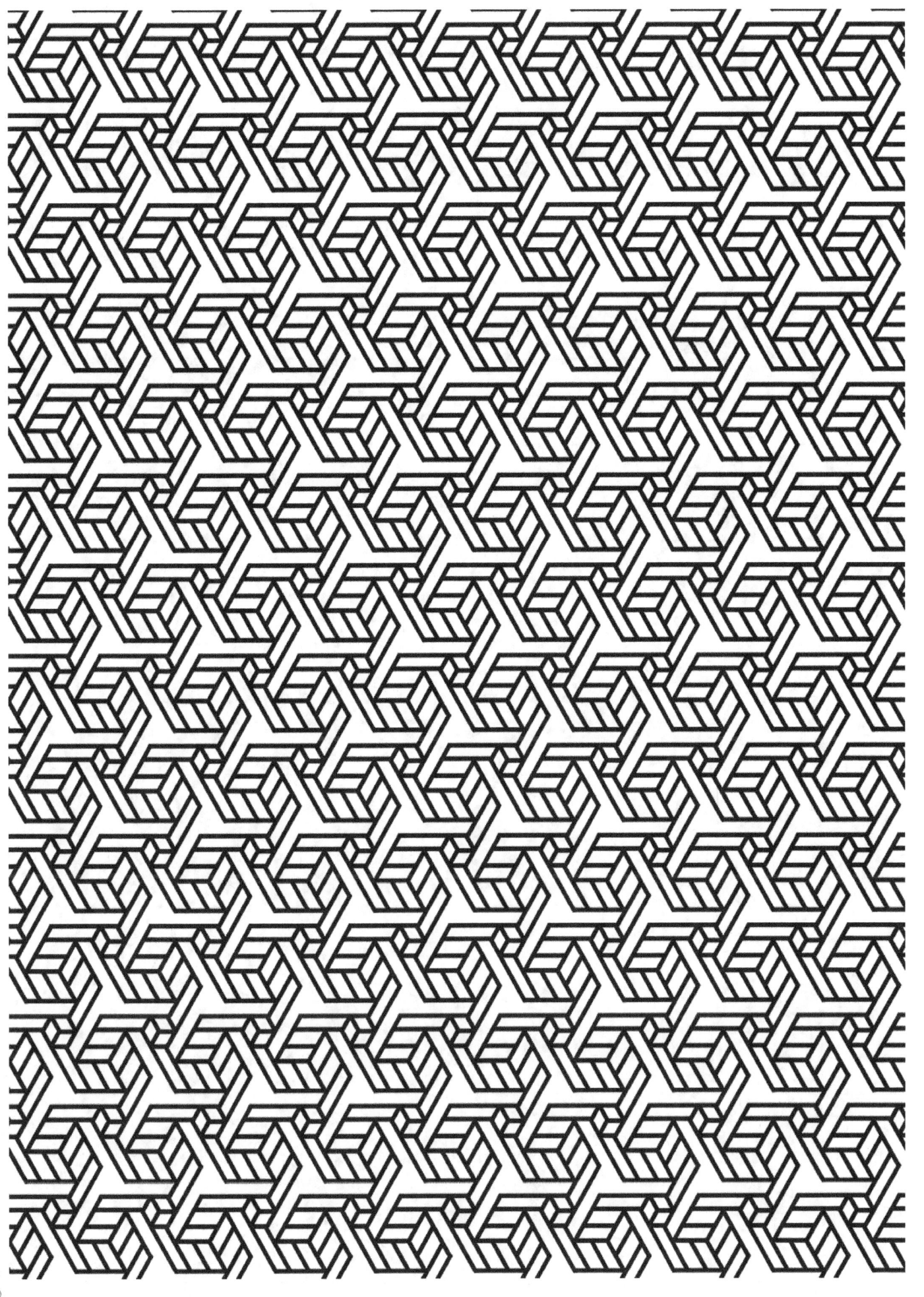

A father is a man who expects his son to be as good a man as he meant to be.

Frank A. Clark

I know that I will never find my father in any other man who comes into my life, because it is a void in my life that can only be filled by him.

Halle Berry

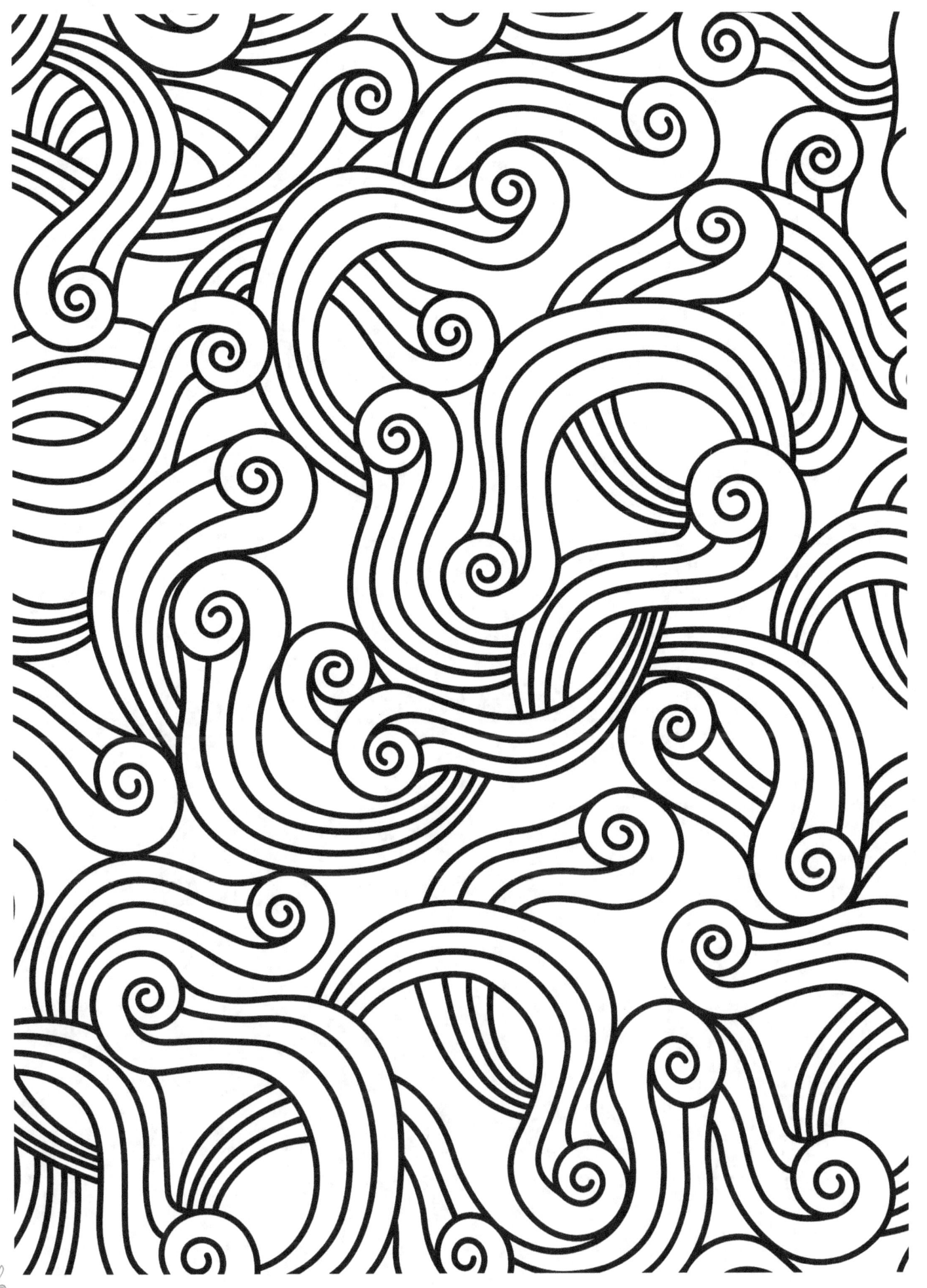

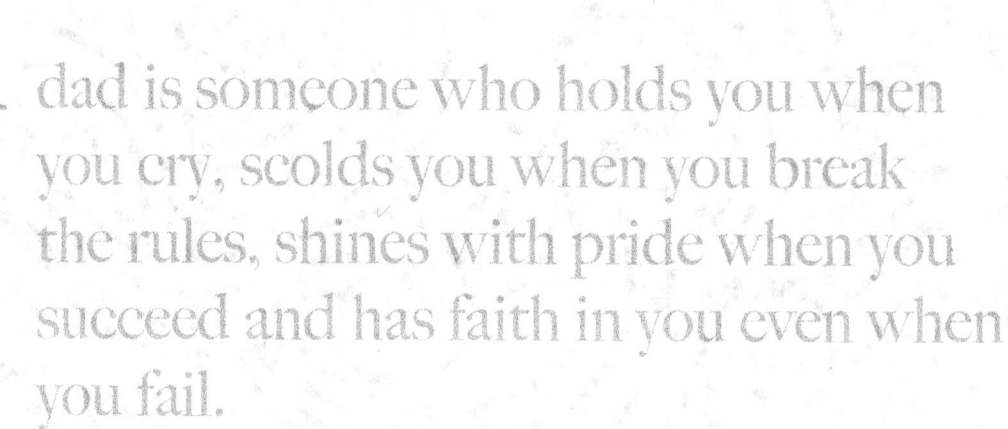

A dad is someone who holds you when you cry, scolds you when you break the rules, shines with pride when you succeed and has faith in you even when you fail.

Author unknown

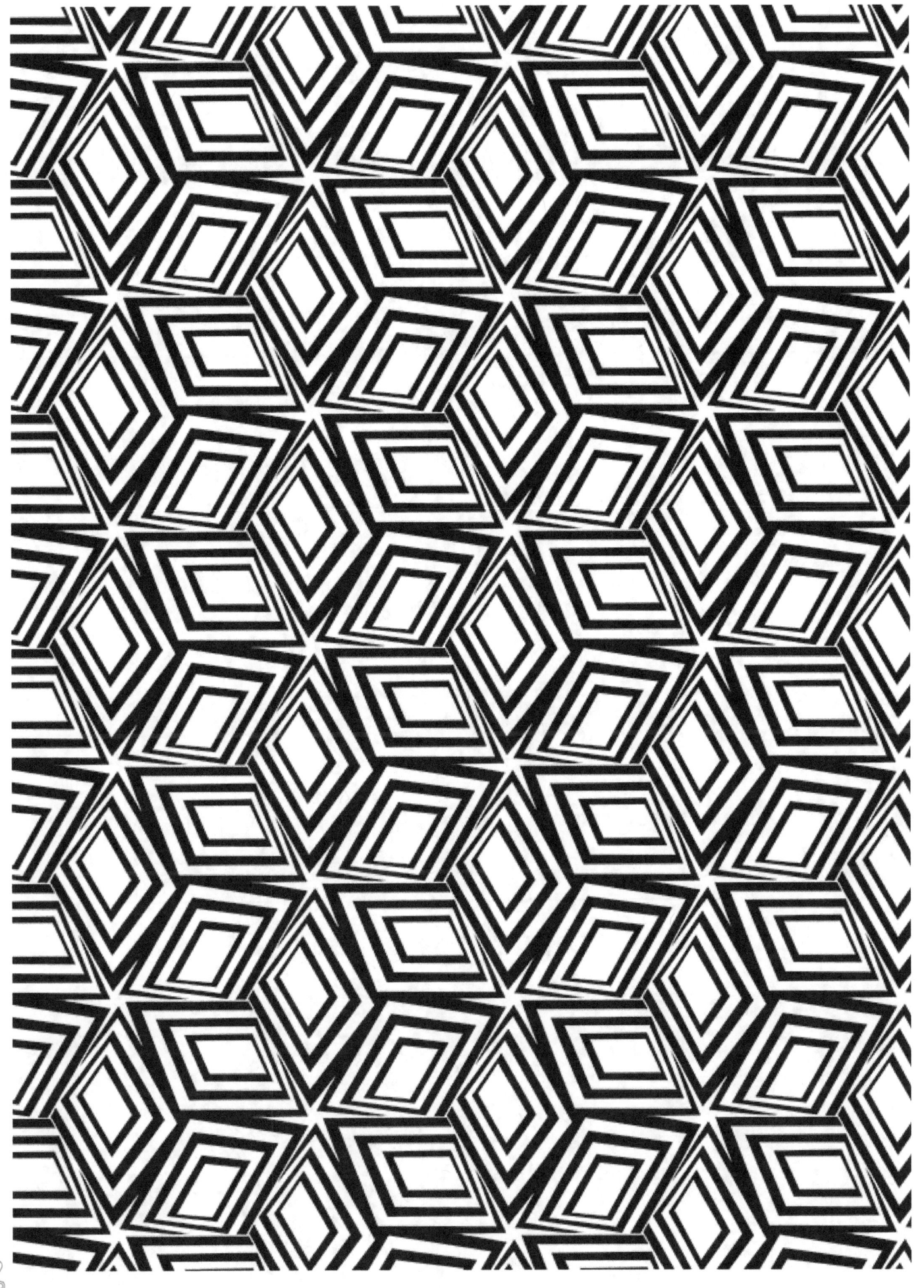

I am not ashamed to say that no man I ever met was my father's equal, and I never loved any other man as much.

Hedy Lamarr

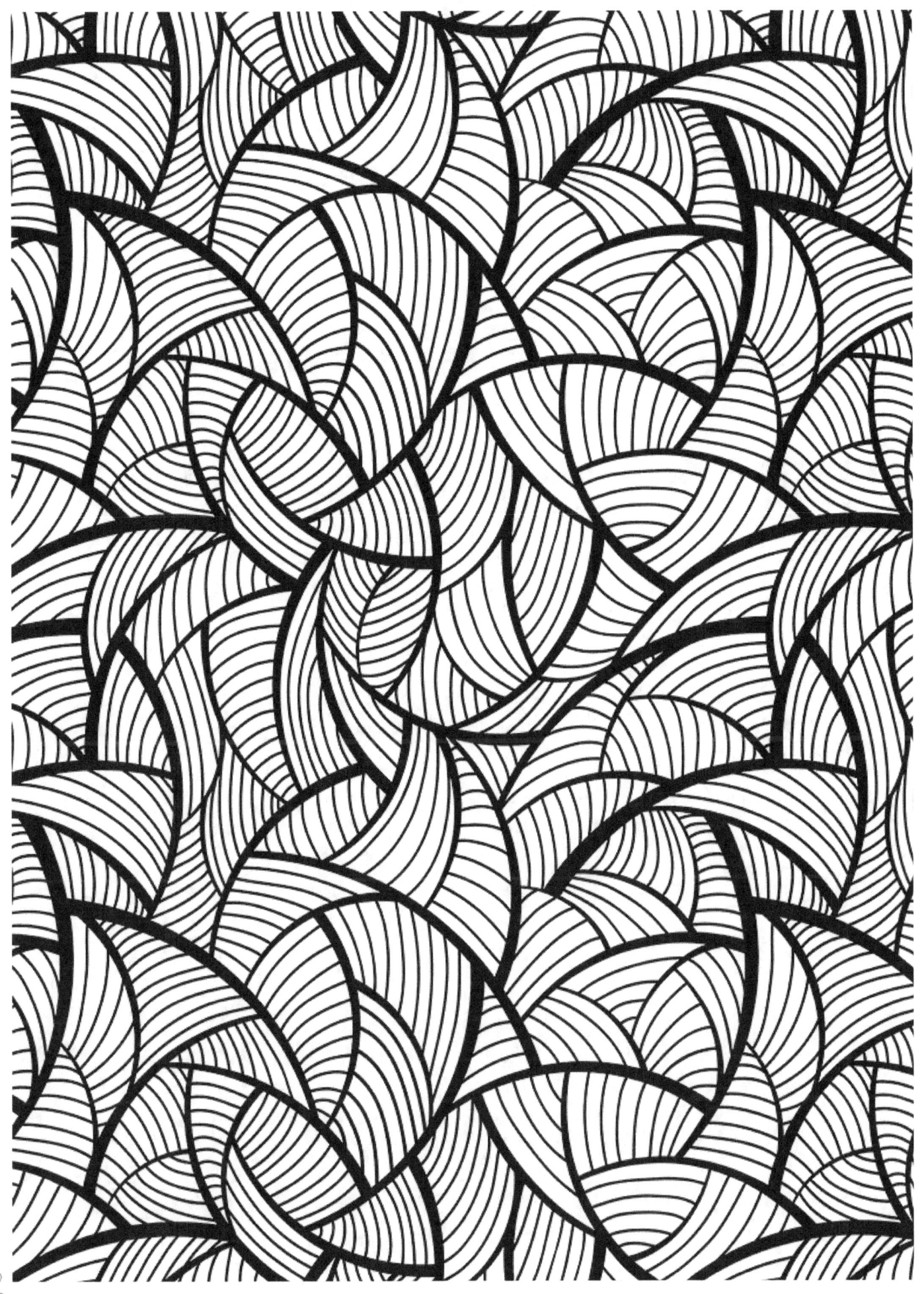

The most important influence in my childhood was my father.

DeForest Kelley

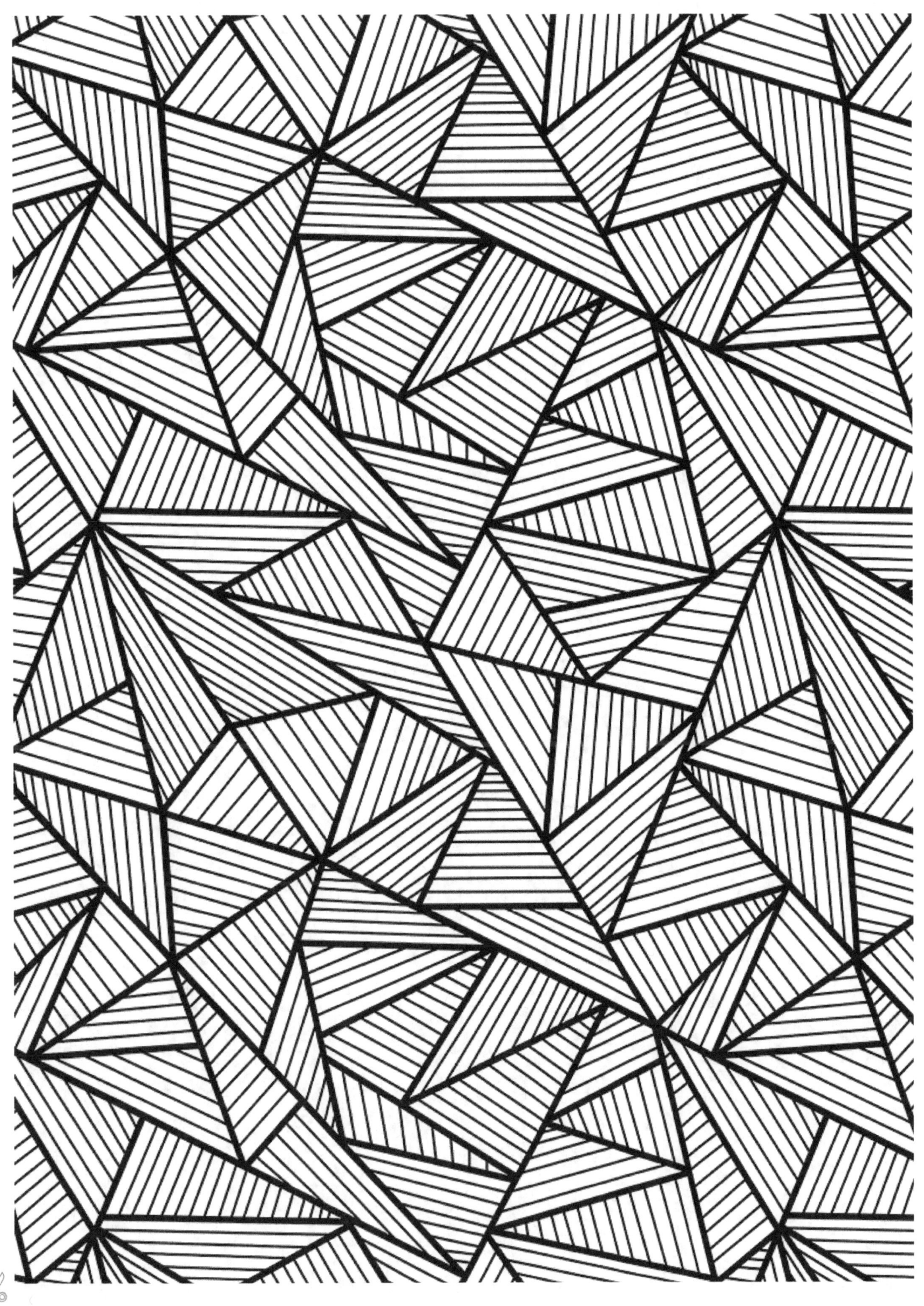

It is easier for a father to have
children than for children to have
a real father.

Pope John XXIII

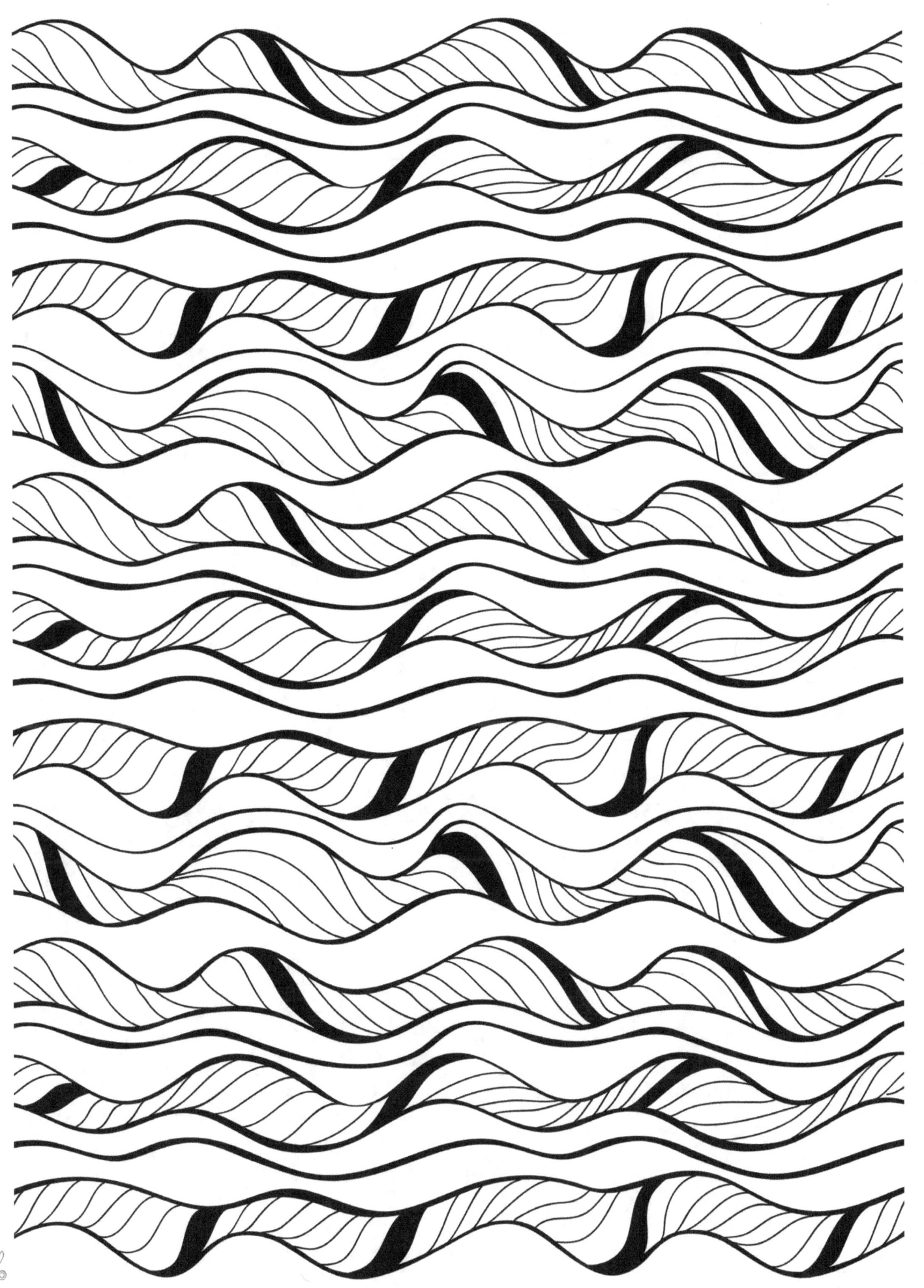

The child is father of the man.

William Wordsworth

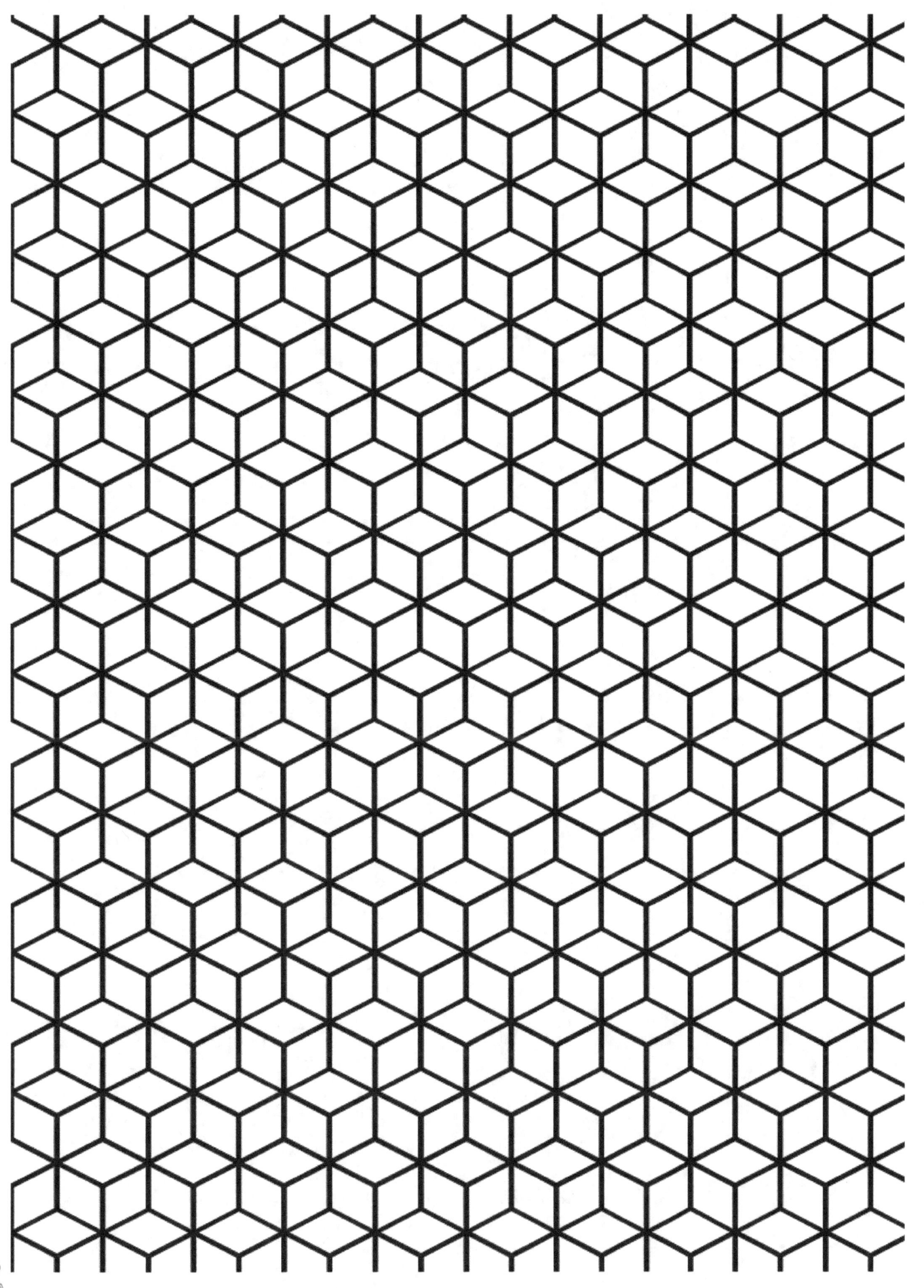

M

y father taught me that the only way you can make good at anything is to practice, and then practice some more.

Pete Rose

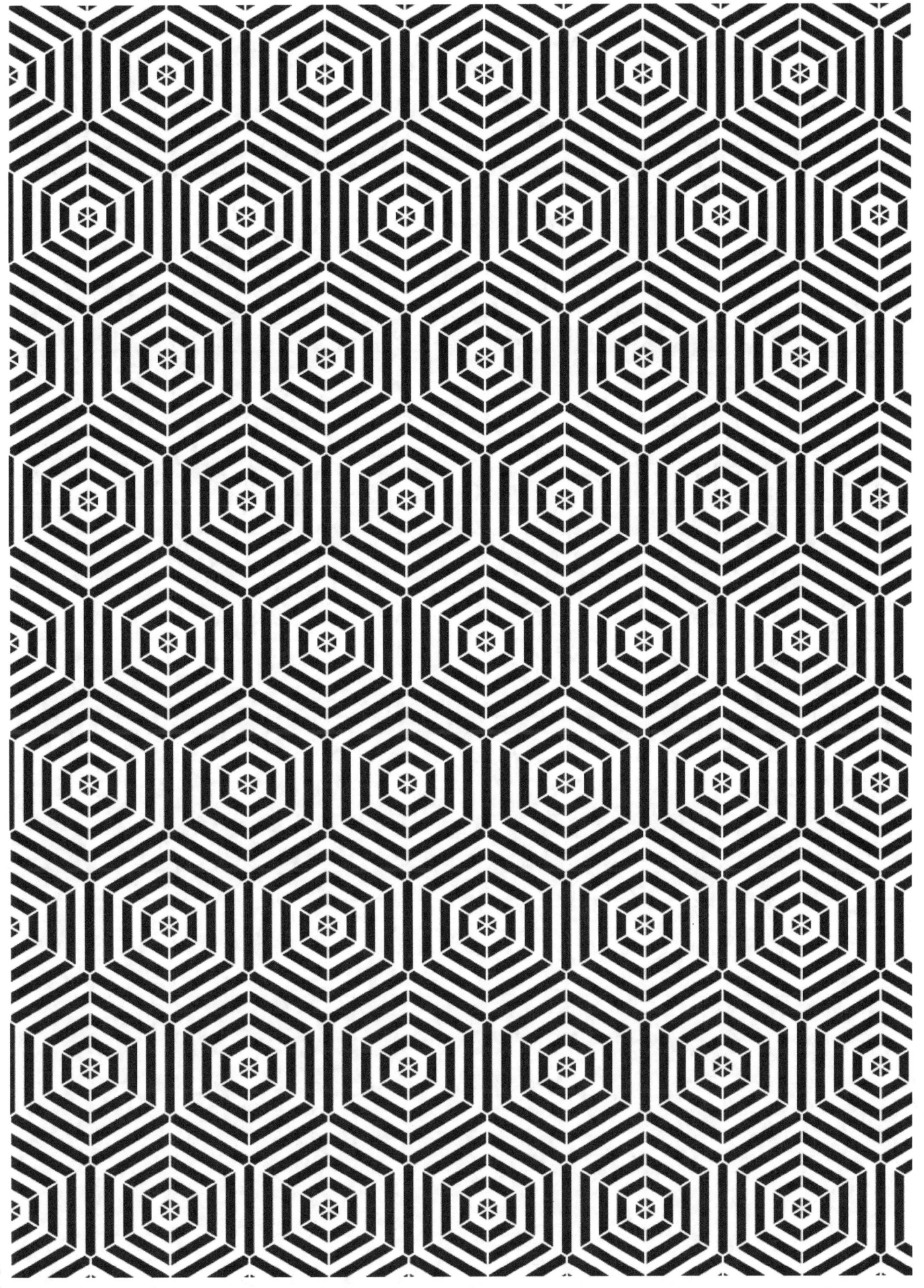

A working definition of fathering might be this: fathering is the act of guiding a child to behave in ways that lead to the child's becoming a secure child in full, thus increasing his or her chances of being happy and fruitful as a young adult.

Clyde Edgerton

When I was 18, I thought my father was pretty dumb. After a while when I got to be 21, I was amazed to find out how much he'd learned in three years.

Frank Butler

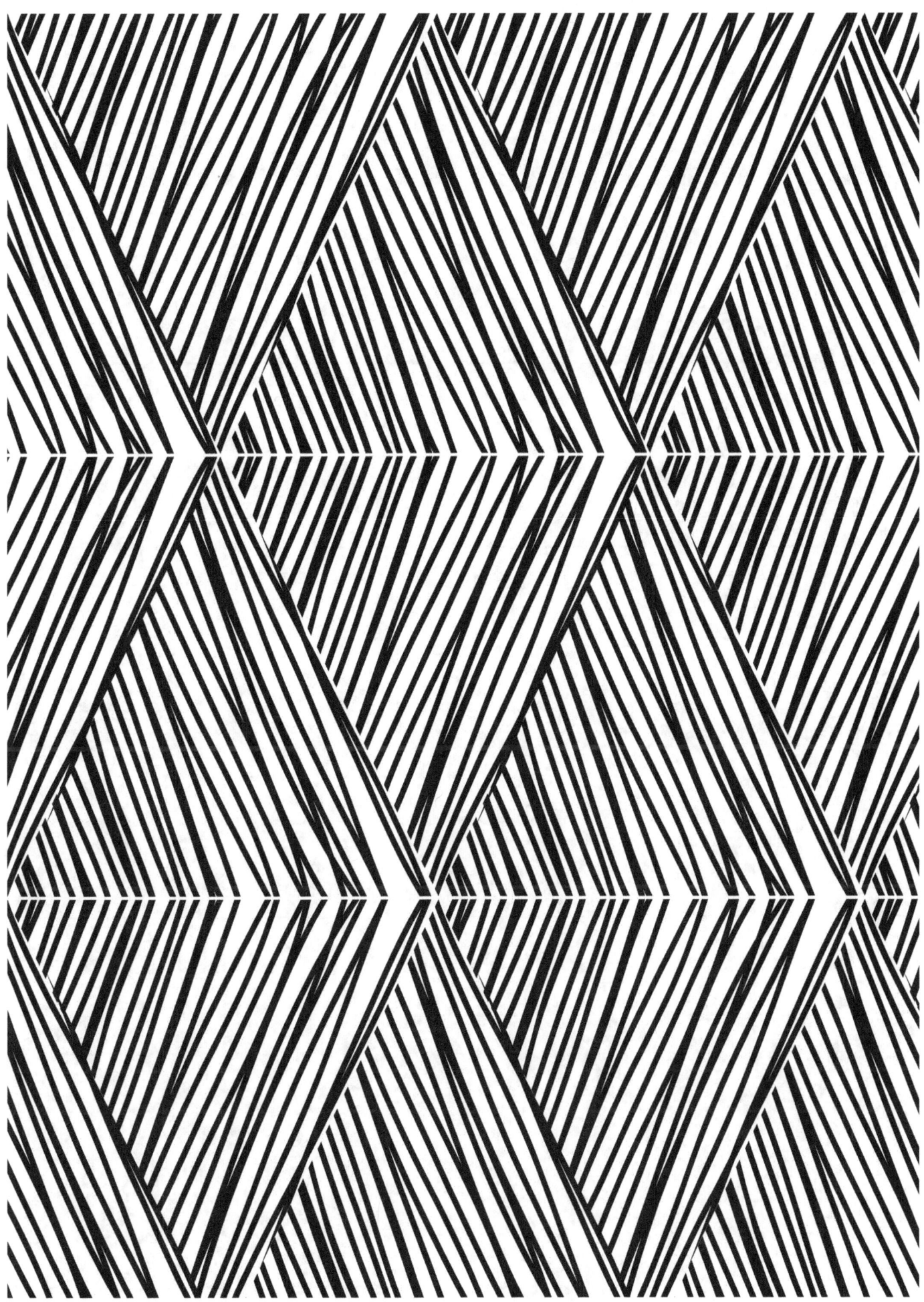

Being a father, being a friend, those are the things that make me feel successful.

William Hurt

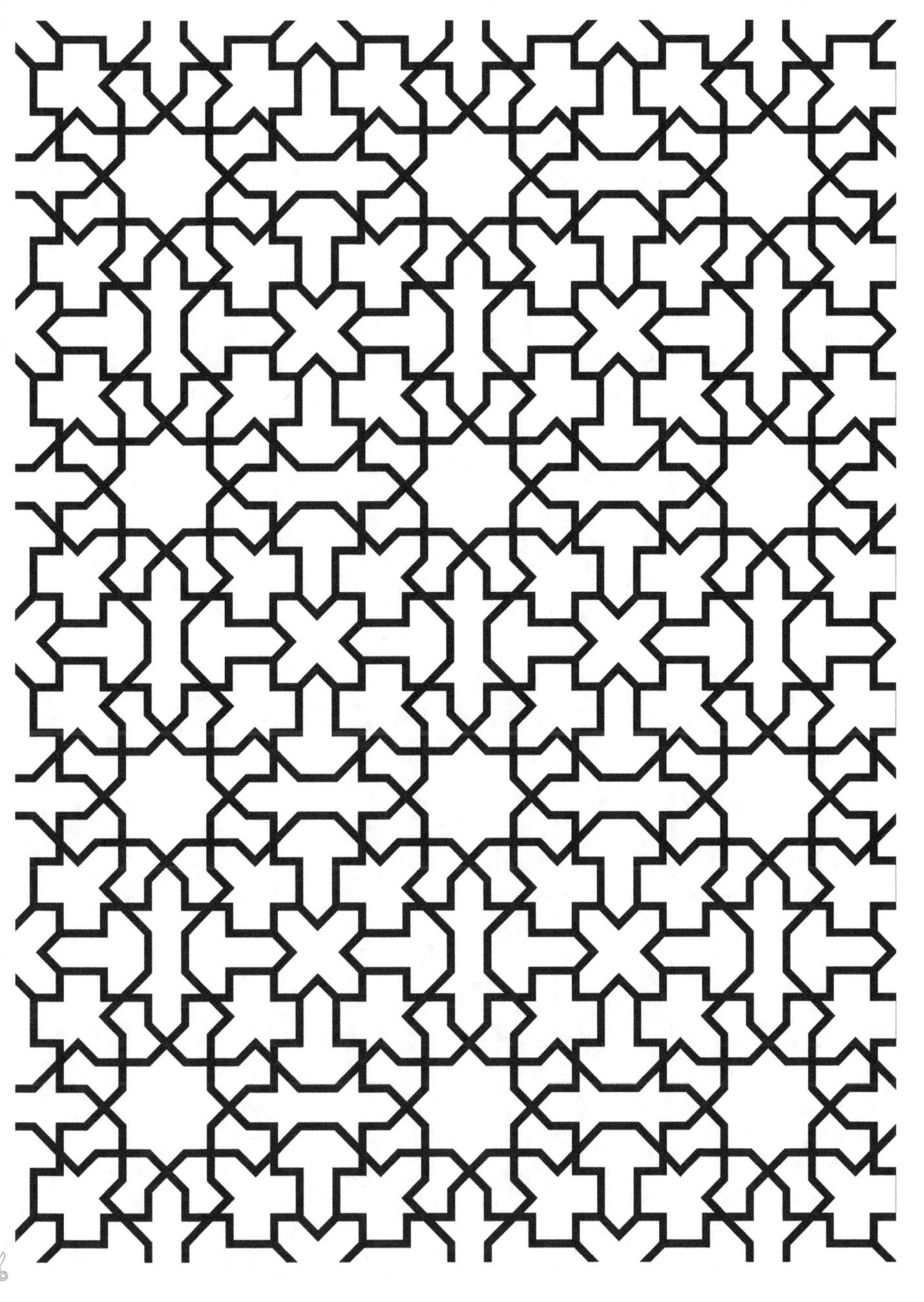

A dad is someone who wants to keep you from making mistakes but instead lets you find your own way, even though his heart breaks in silence when you get hurt.

Author unknown

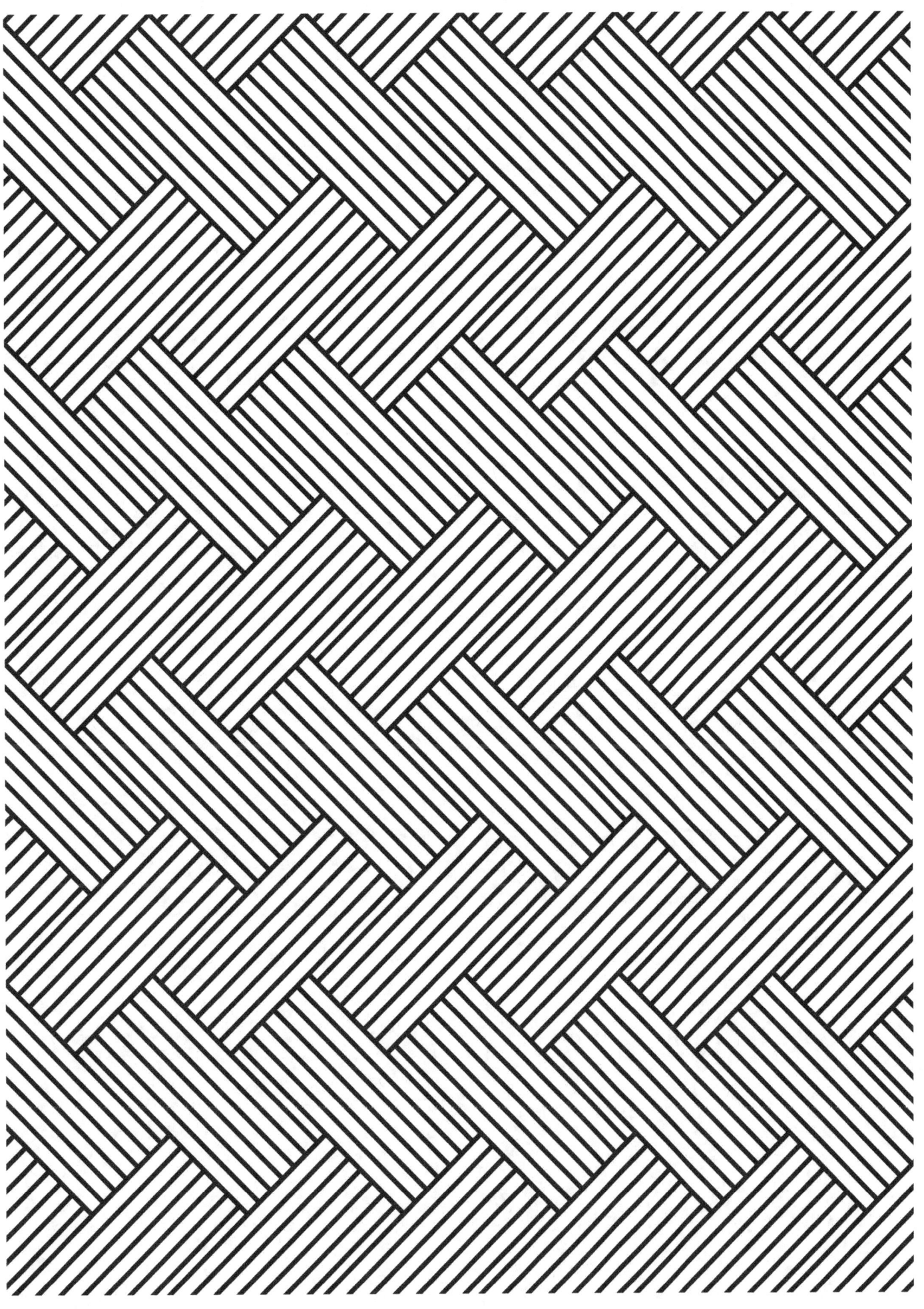

Love and fear. Everything the father of a family says must inspire one or the other.

Joseph Joubert

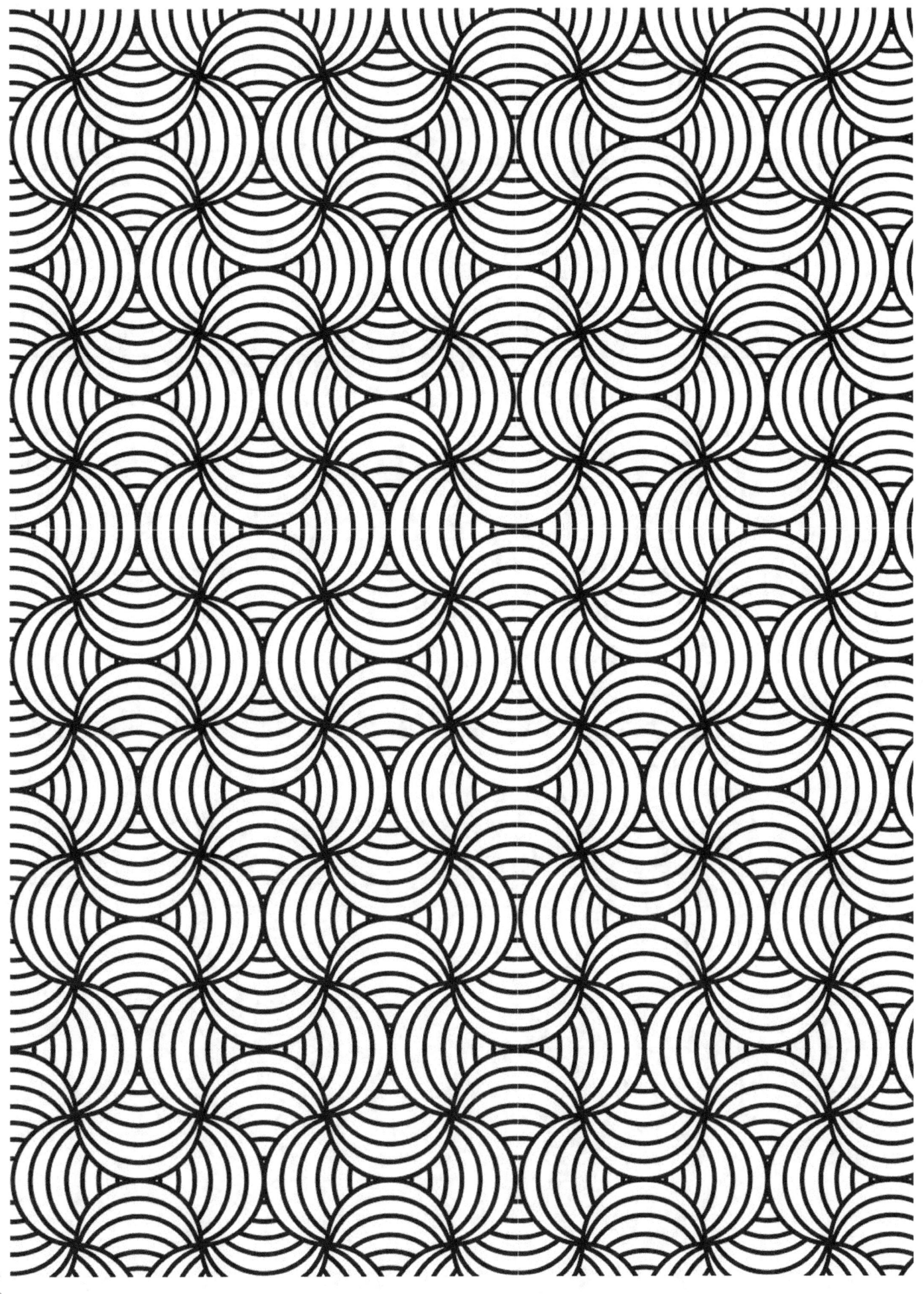

Whoever does not have a good father should procure one.

Friedrich Nietzsche

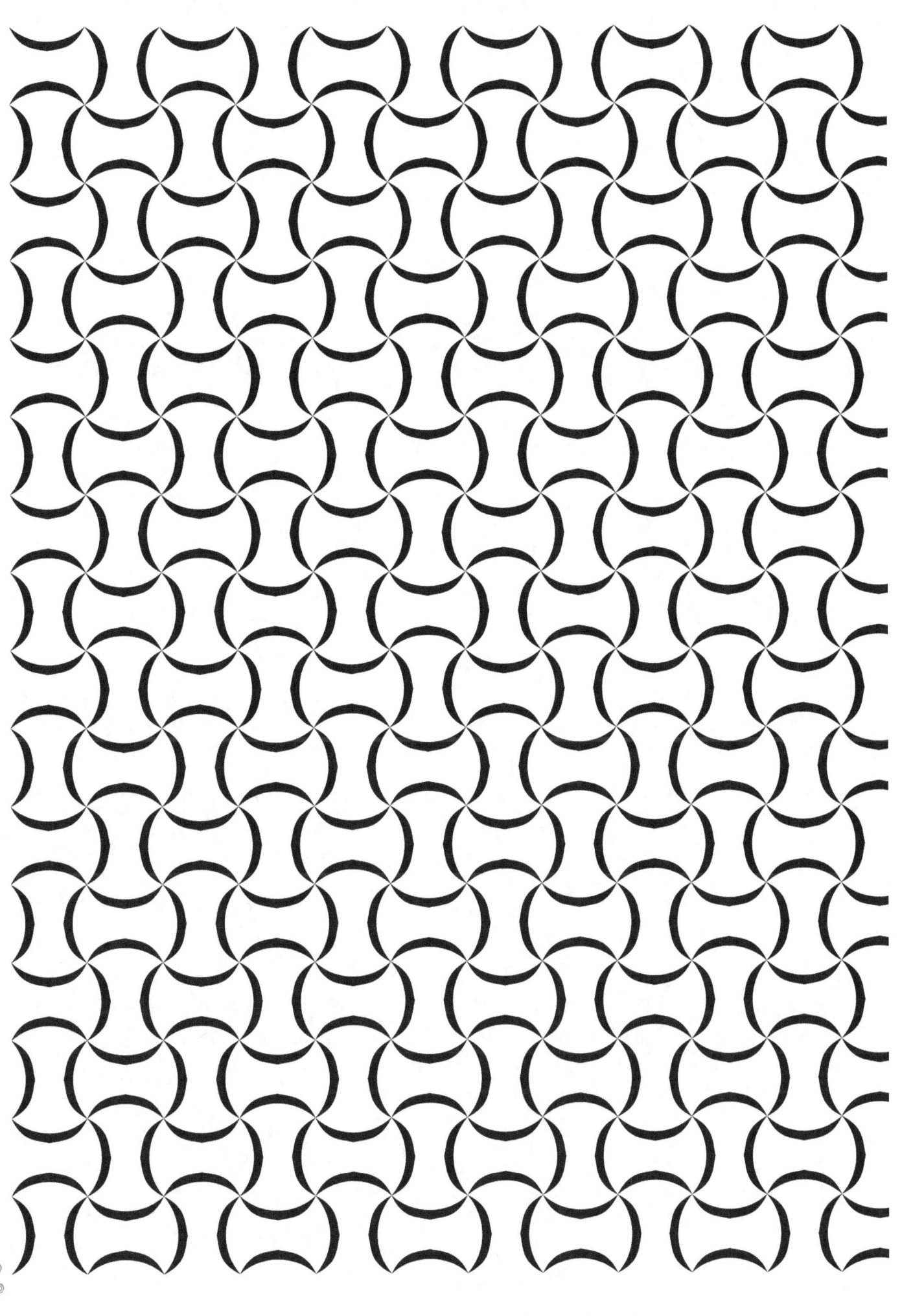

Every parent is at some time the father of the unreturned prodigal, with nothing to do but keep his house open to hope.

John Ciardi

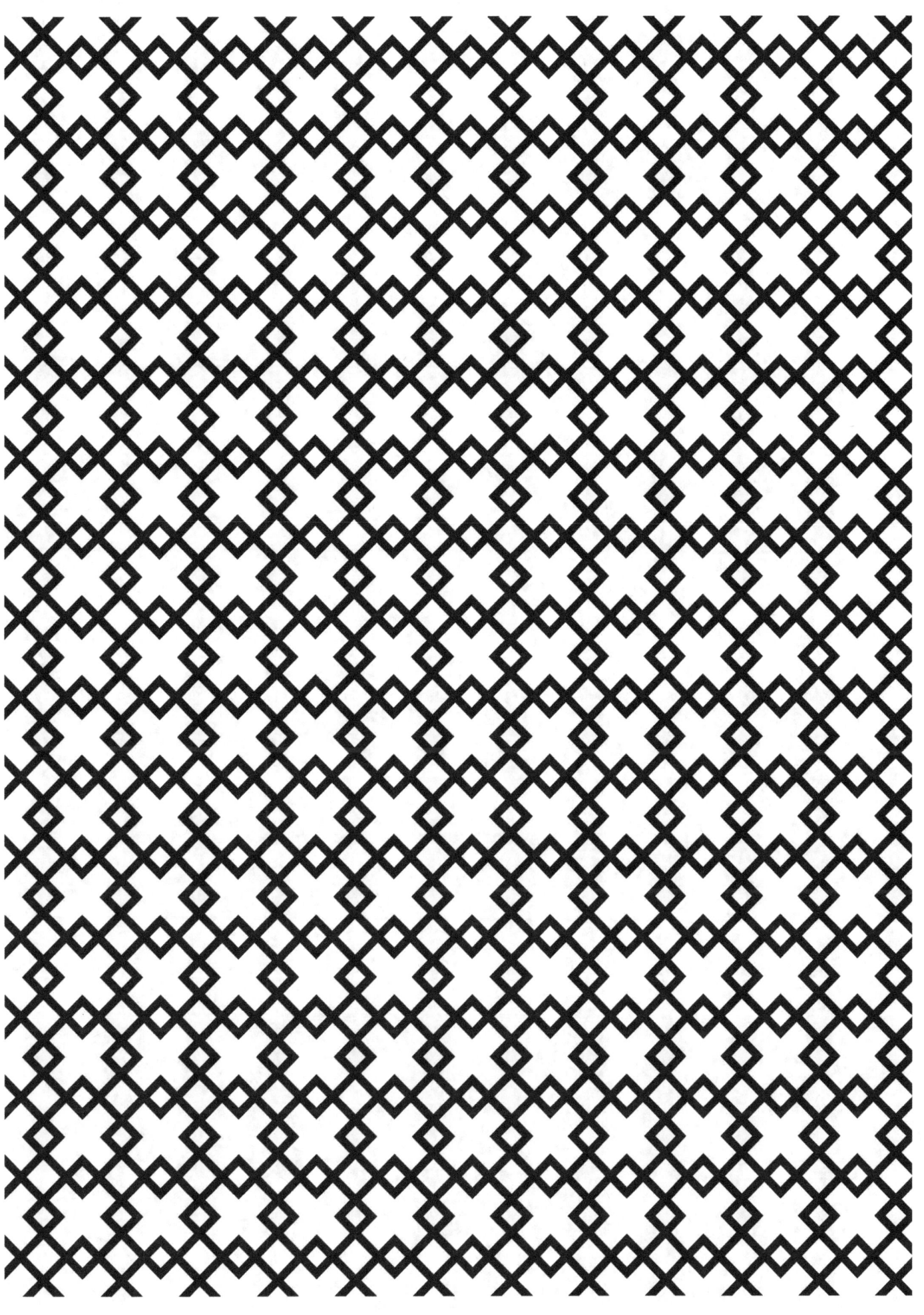

M

y father gave me the greatest gift anyone could give another person, he believed in me.

Jim Valvano

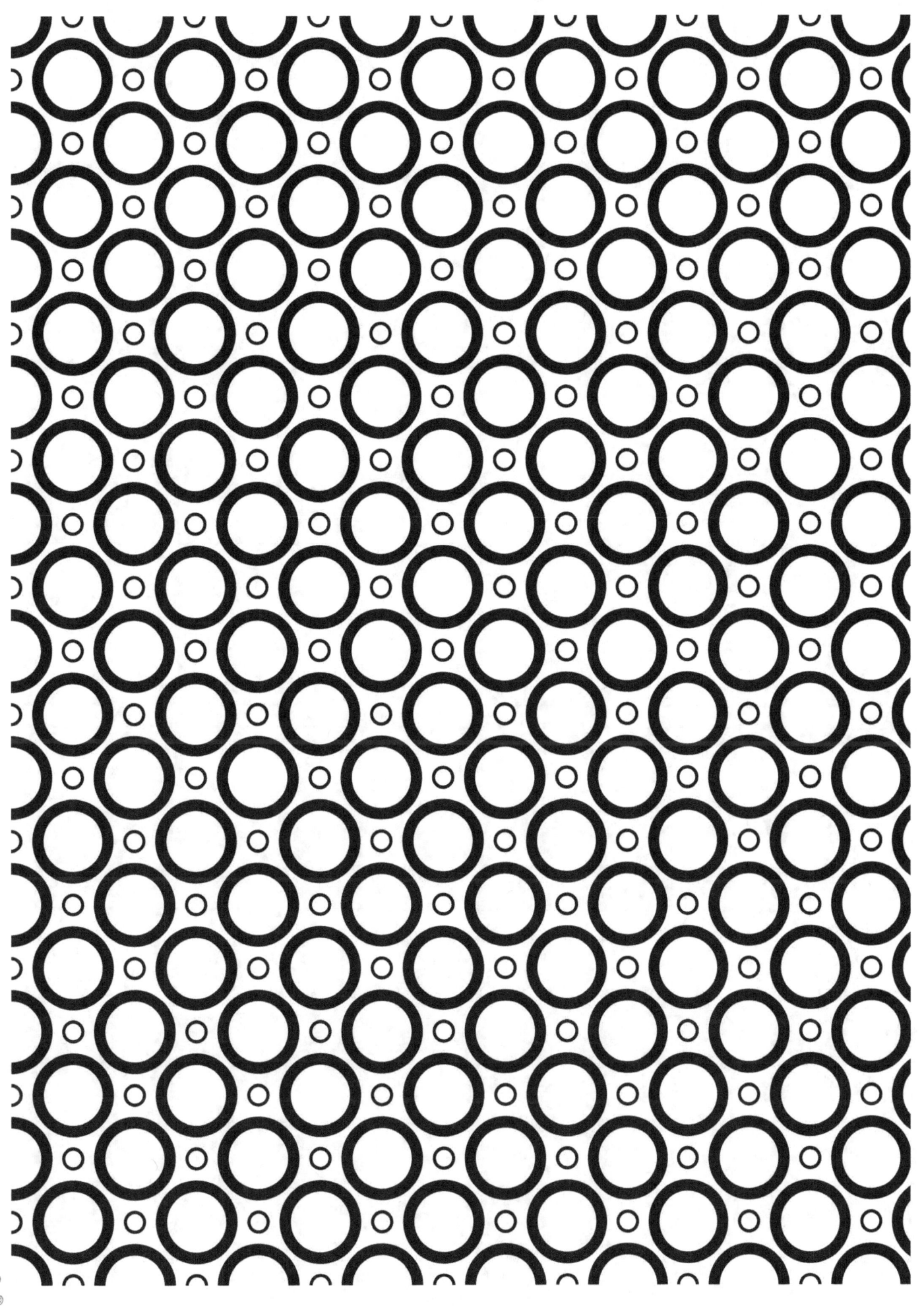

A dad is someone who
wants to catch you before you fall
but instead picks you up,
brushes you off,
and lets you try again.

Author unknown

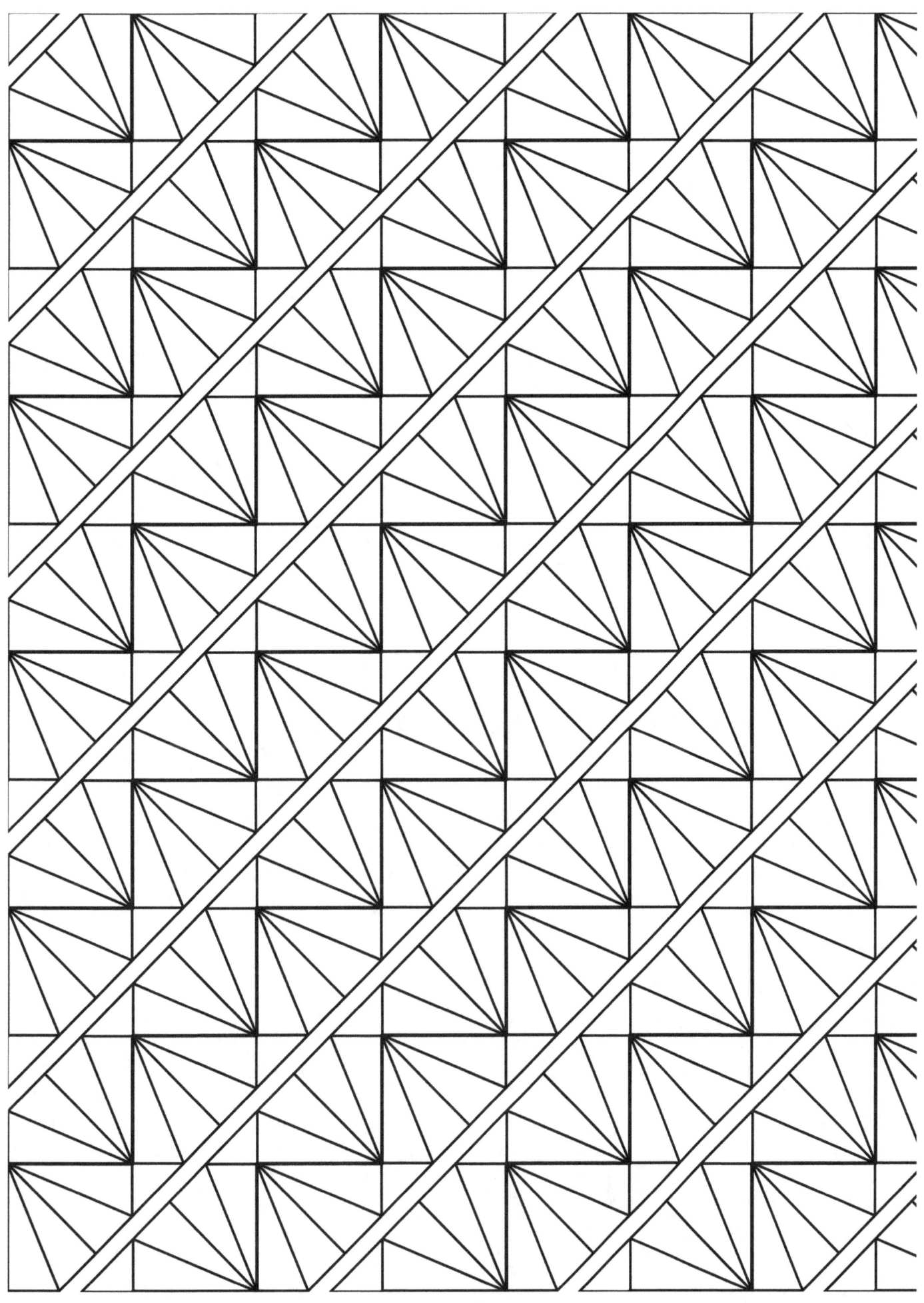

I cannot think of any need in childhood as strong as the need for a father's protection.

Sigmund Freud

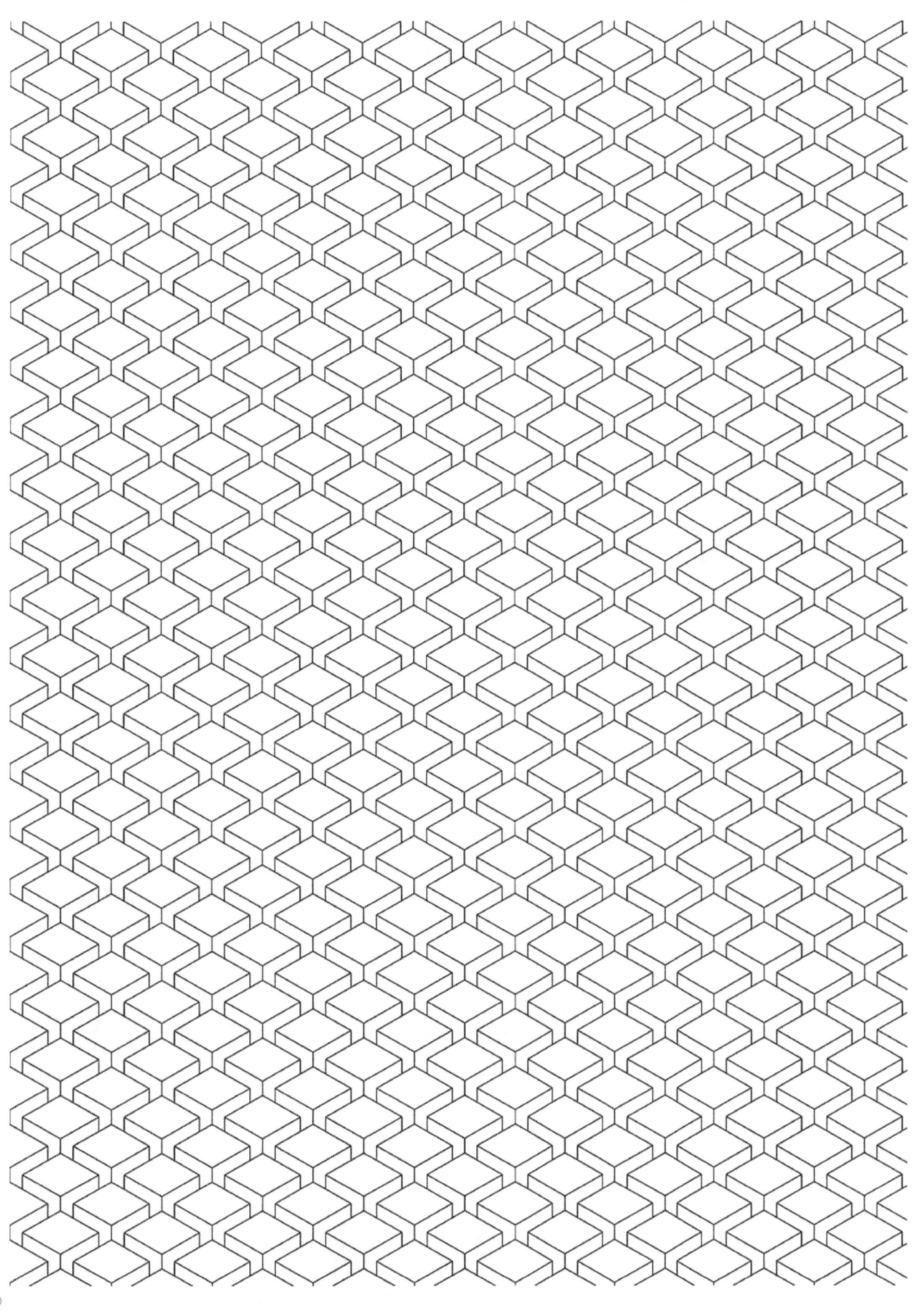

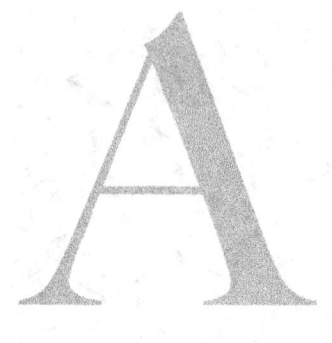father is the one man who will never give up on you.

Author unknown

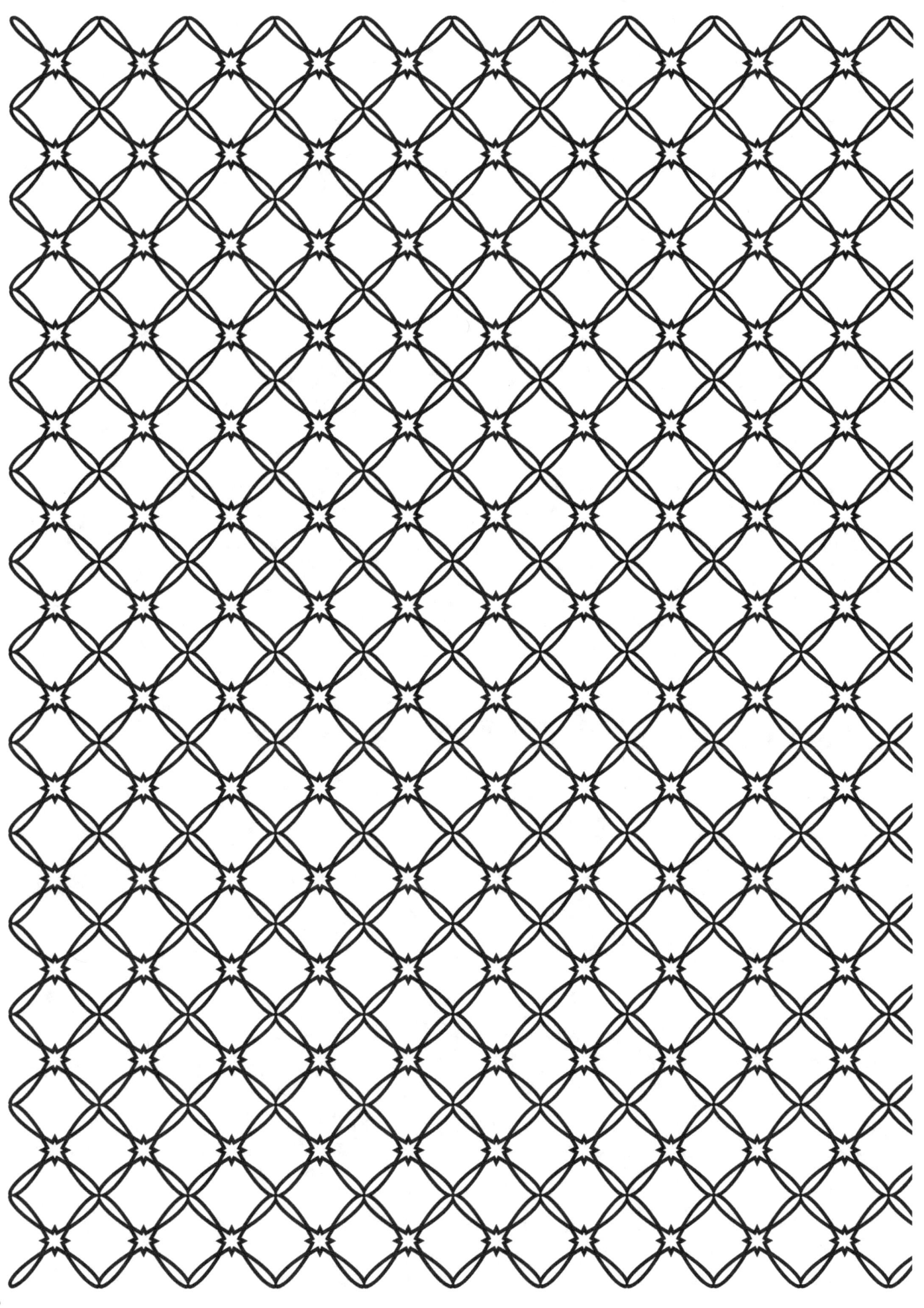

A father is someone who carries pictures in his wallet where his money used to be.

Author unknown

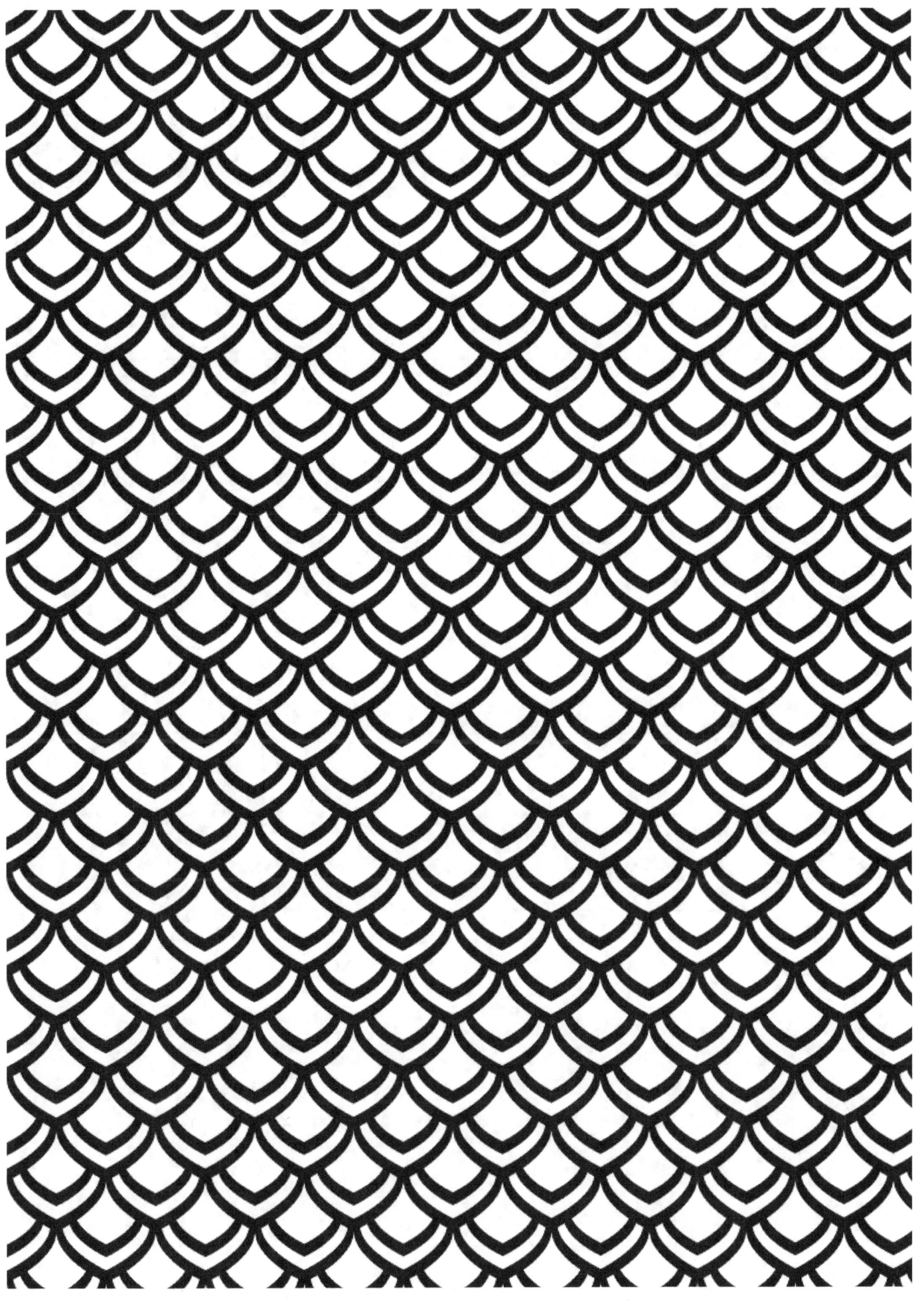

I think that the best thing we can do for our children is to allow them to do things for themselves, allow them to be strong, allow them to experience life on their own terms.

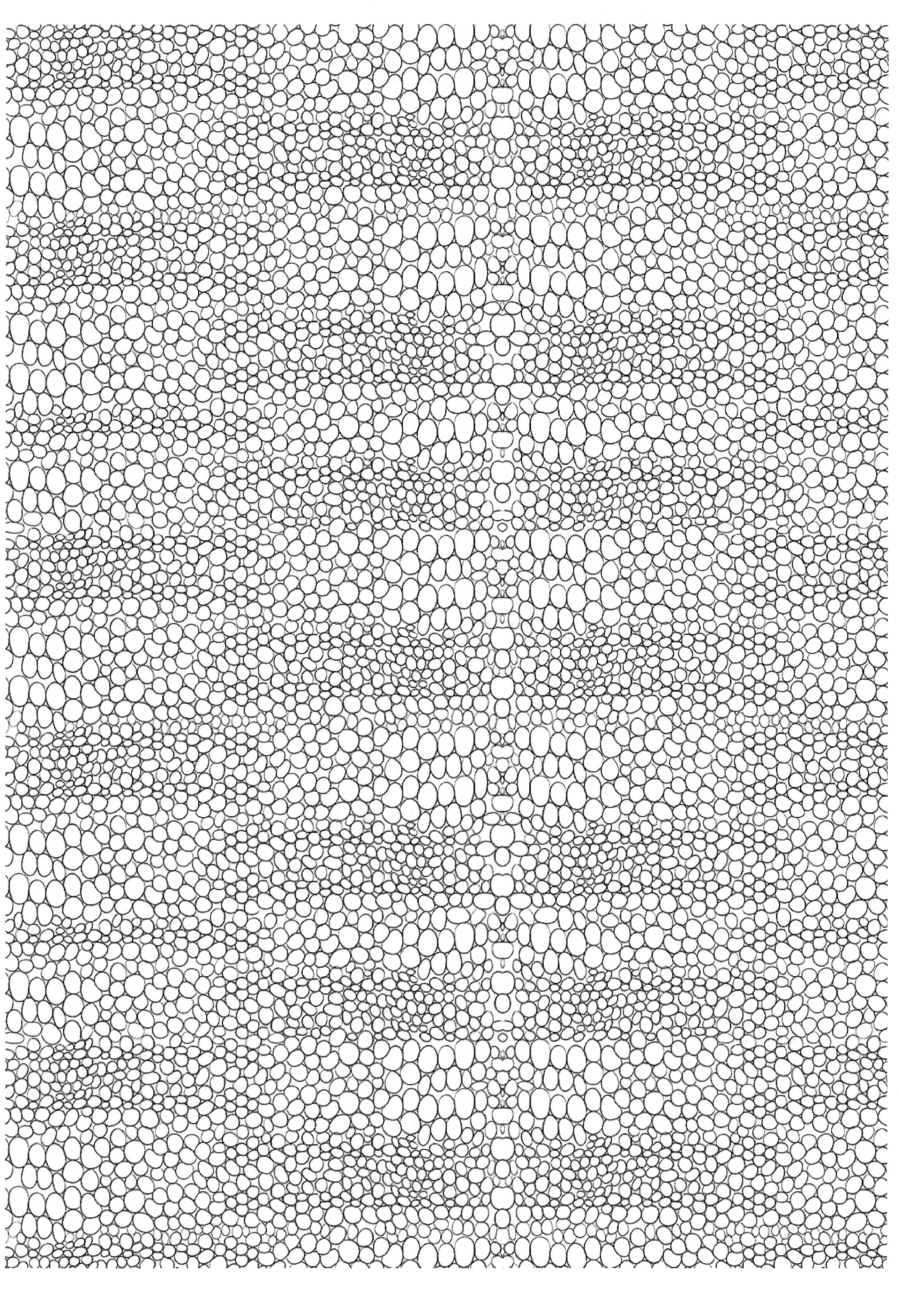

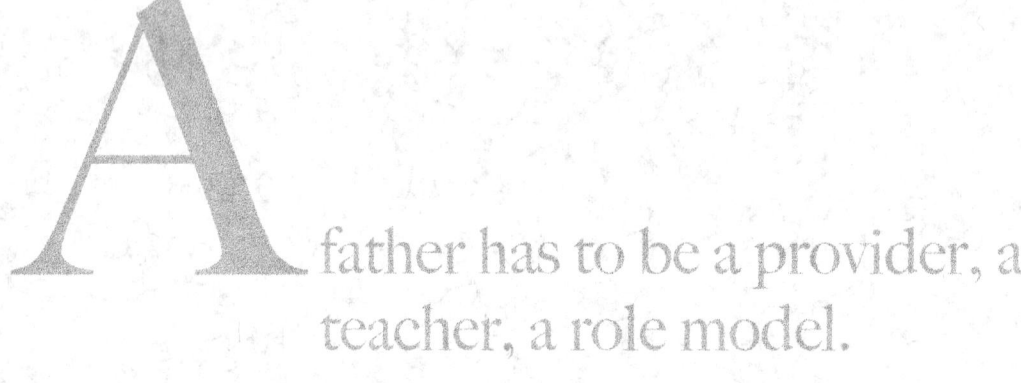

A father has to be a provider, a teacher, a role model.

Stephen Colbert

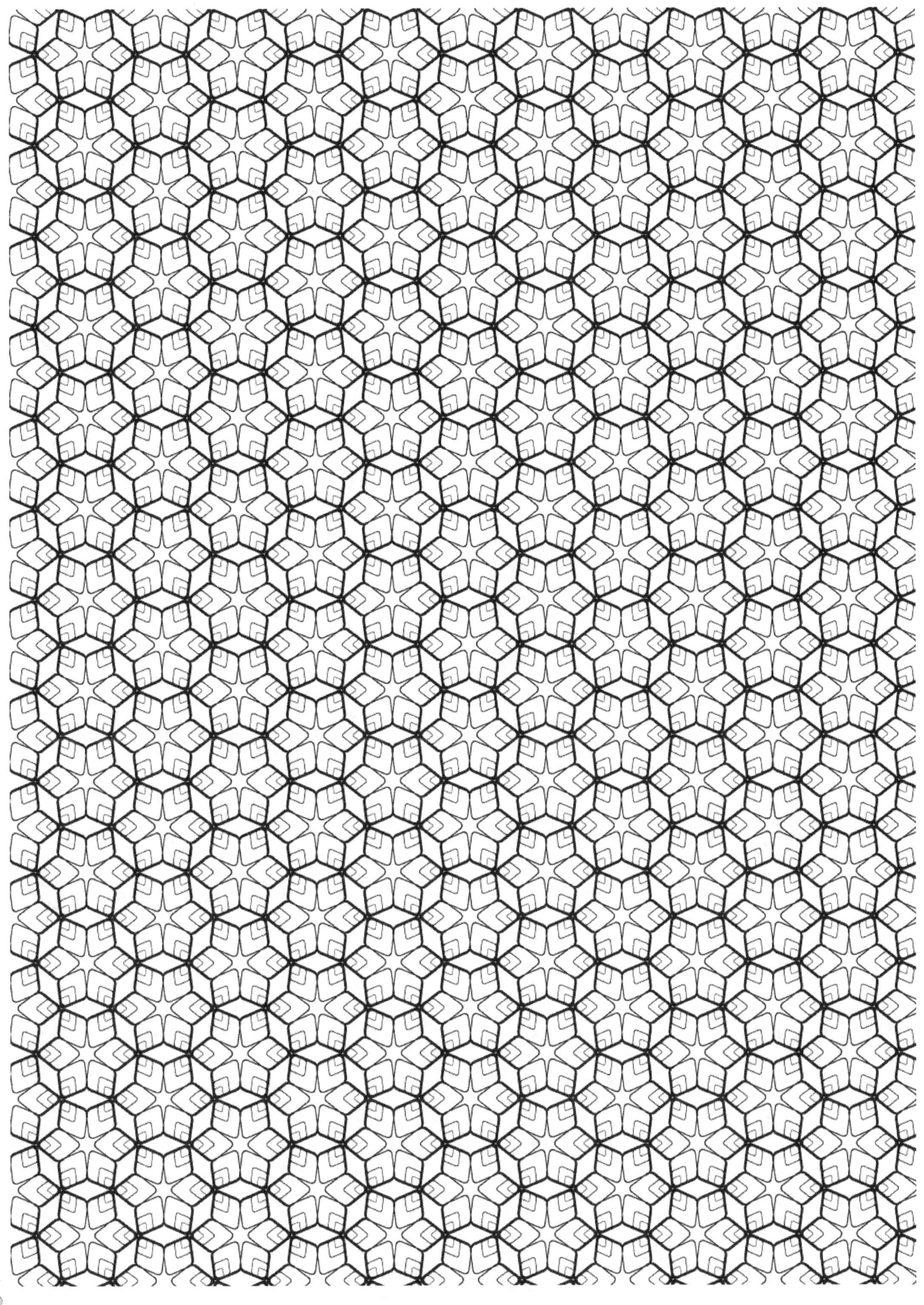

The heart of a father is the masterpiece of nature.

Antoine François Prévost

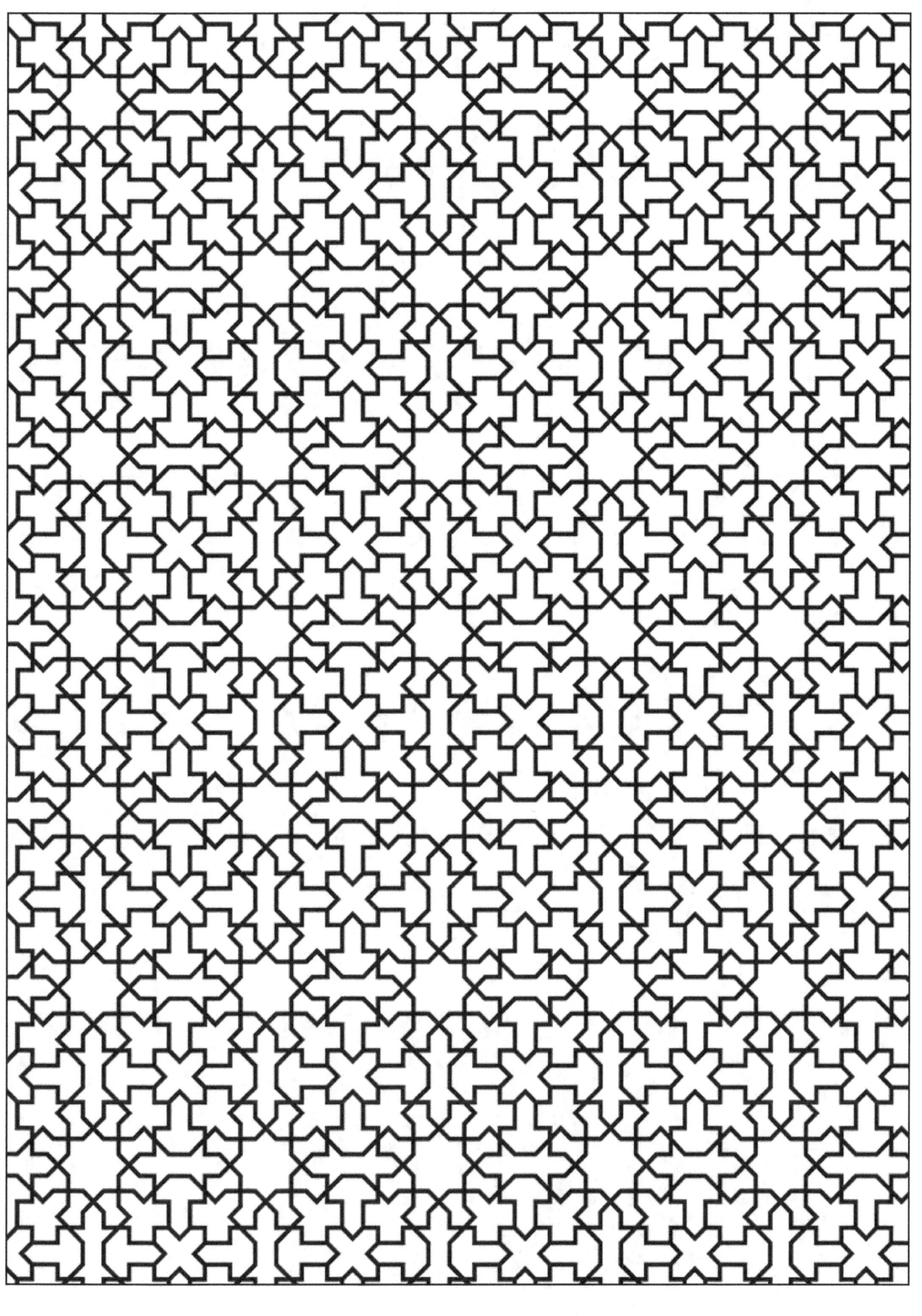

There are times a man has to do things he doesn't like to, in order to protect his family.

Ralph Moody

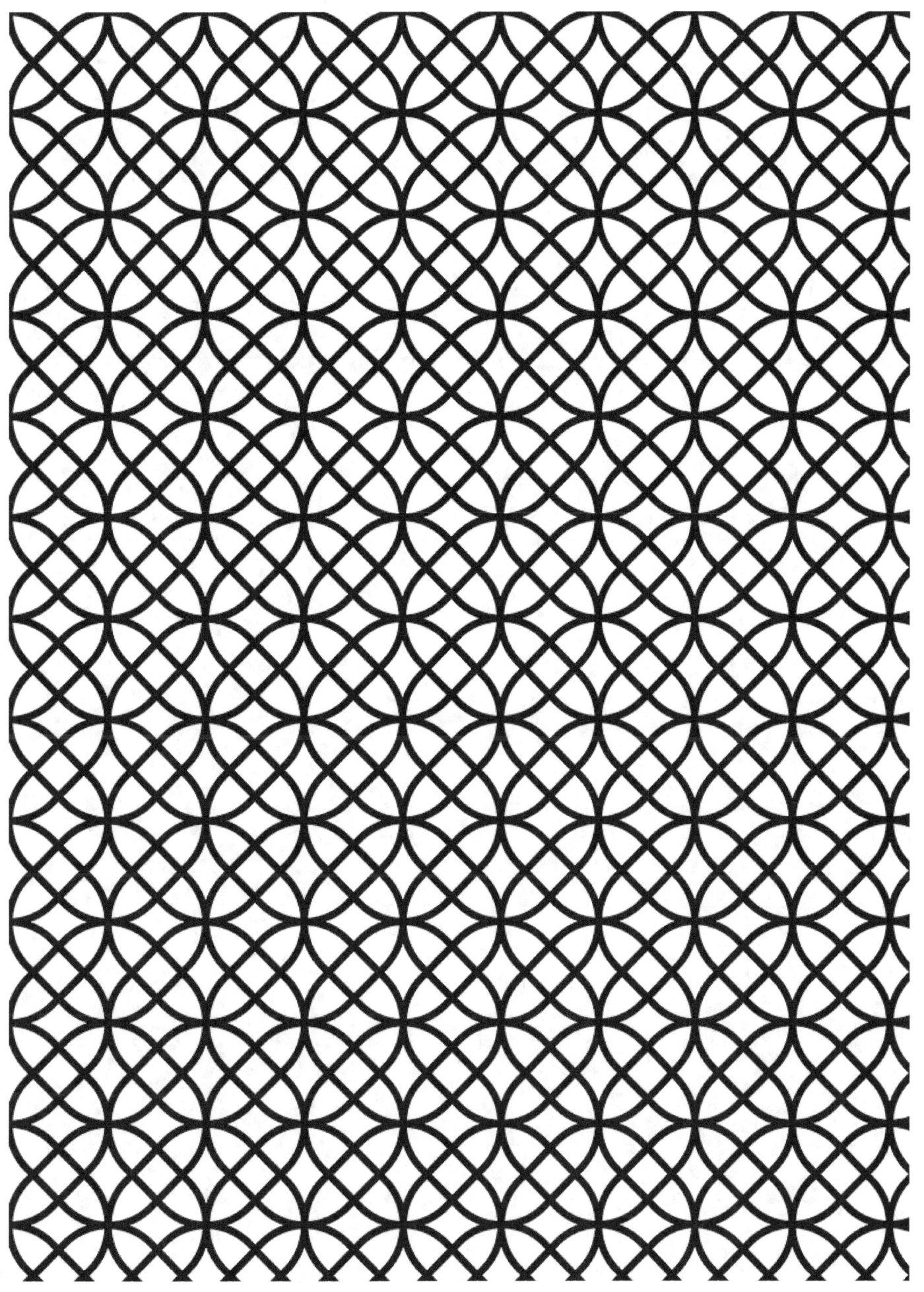

Saturday mornings, I've learned, are a great opportunity for kids to sneak into your bed, fall back asleep, and kick you in the face.

Dan Pearce

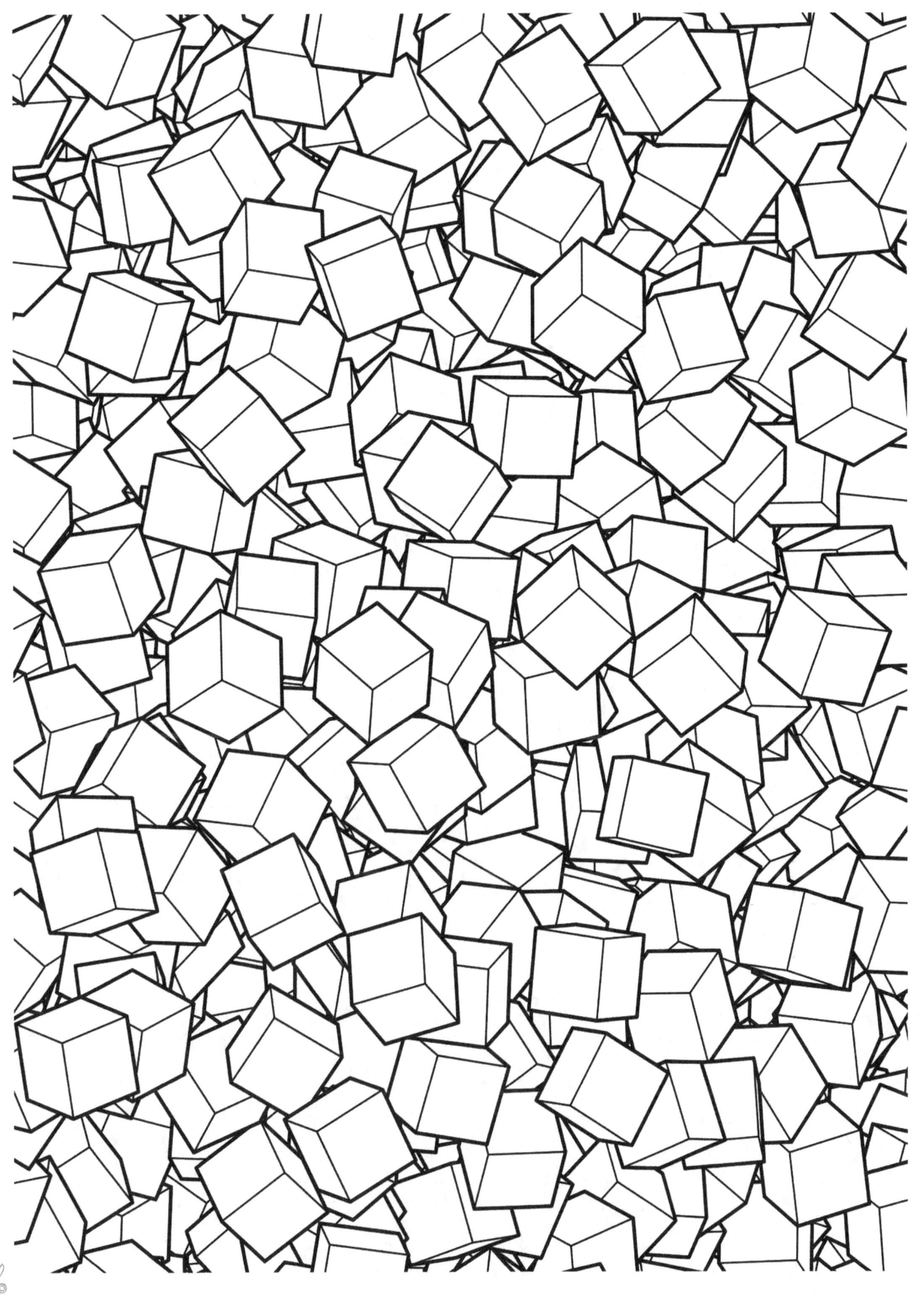

The greatest investment you can do in your life is in gaining time.

Pratik Patil

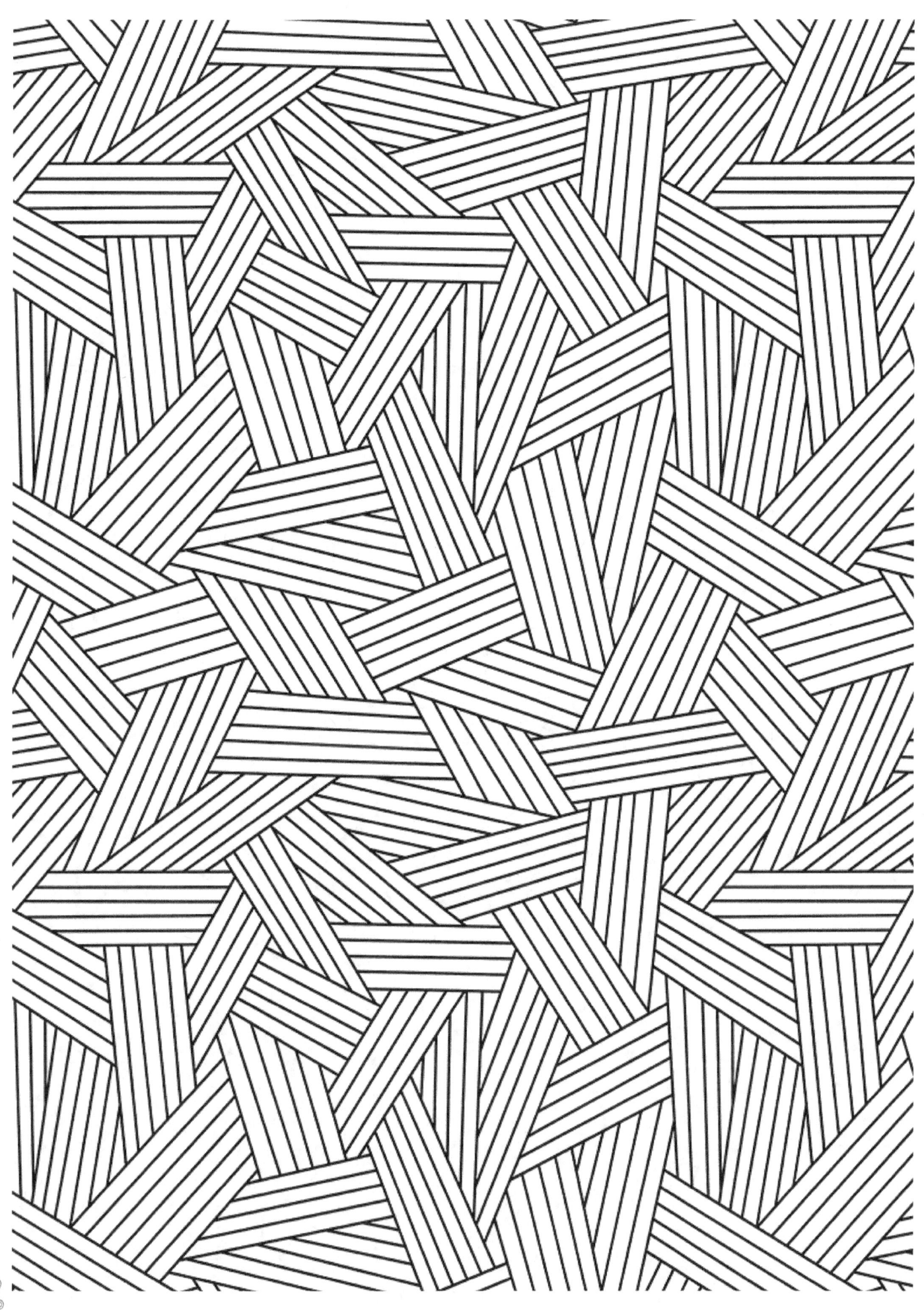

There is a humility of being a father to someone so powerful, as if he were only a narrow conduit for another, greater thing.

Anthony Doerr

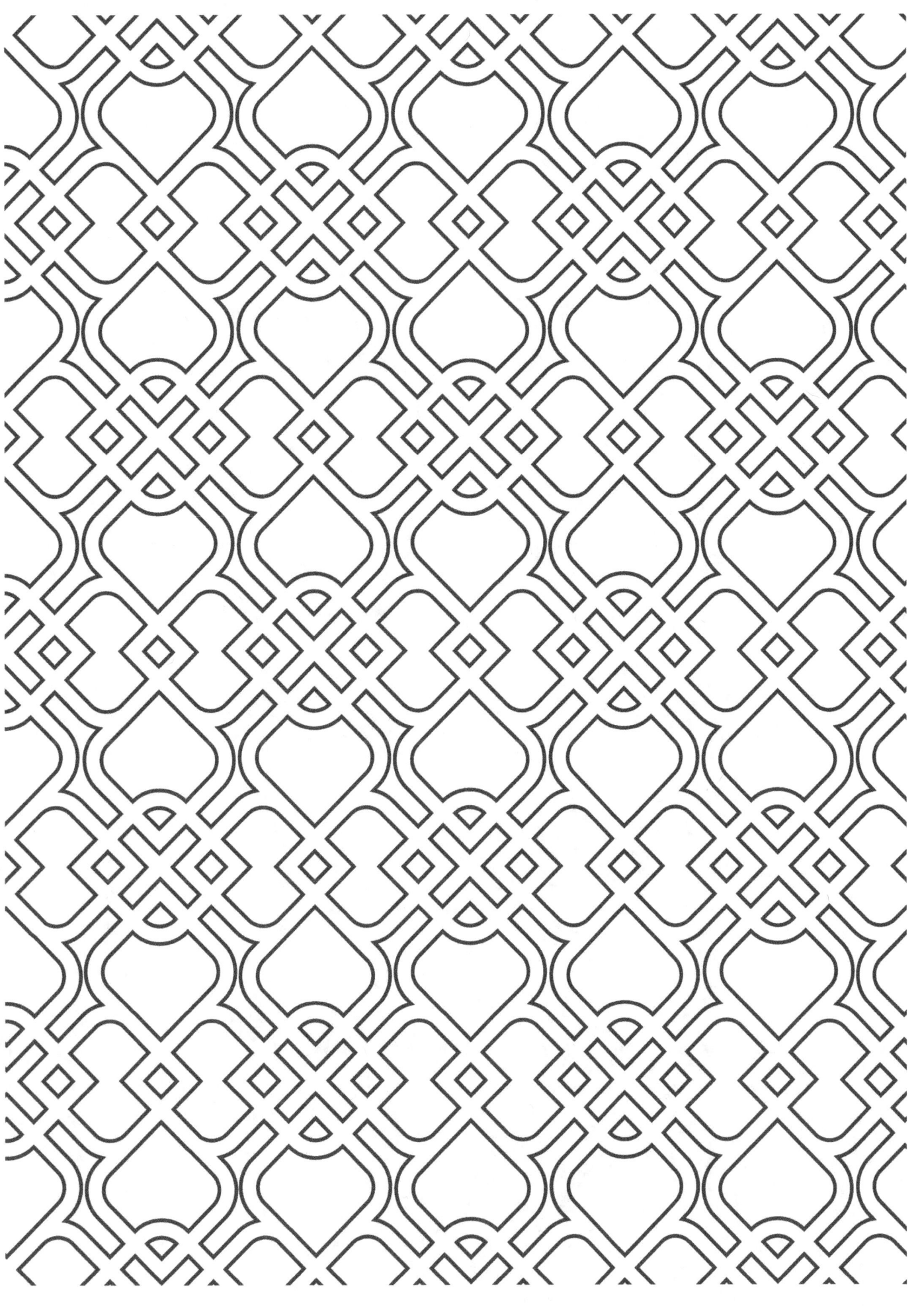

With children the clock is reset. We forget what came before.

Jhumpa Lahiri

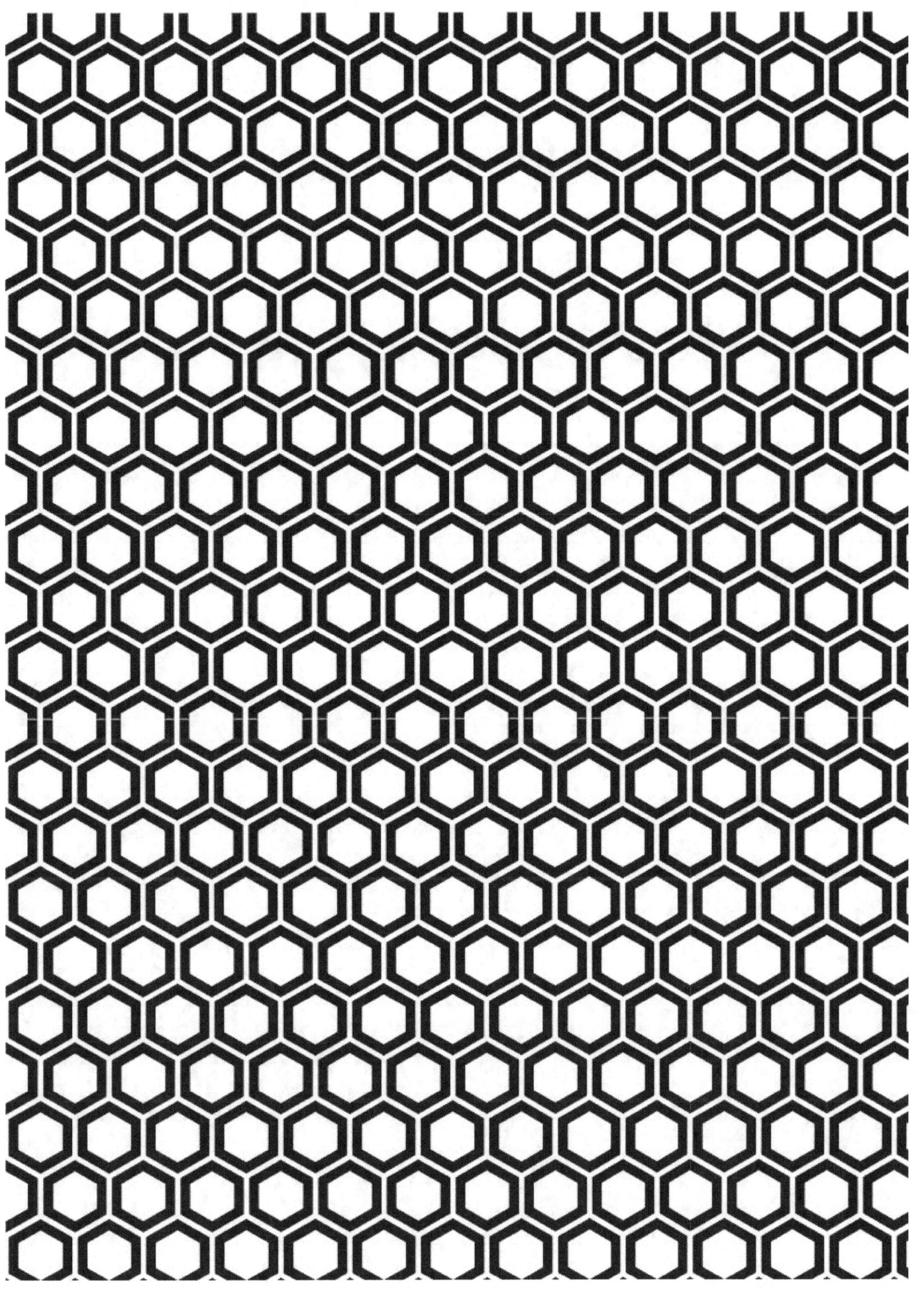

Being a good father to our children
requires a few goals:
Be an example of personal
responsibility
Display self-respect
Be an example of personal
growth, passion, and perseverance
Recognize and accept your child's
particular gifts and nurture them,
not wish they had others
Love and respect your wife

Charles F. Glassman

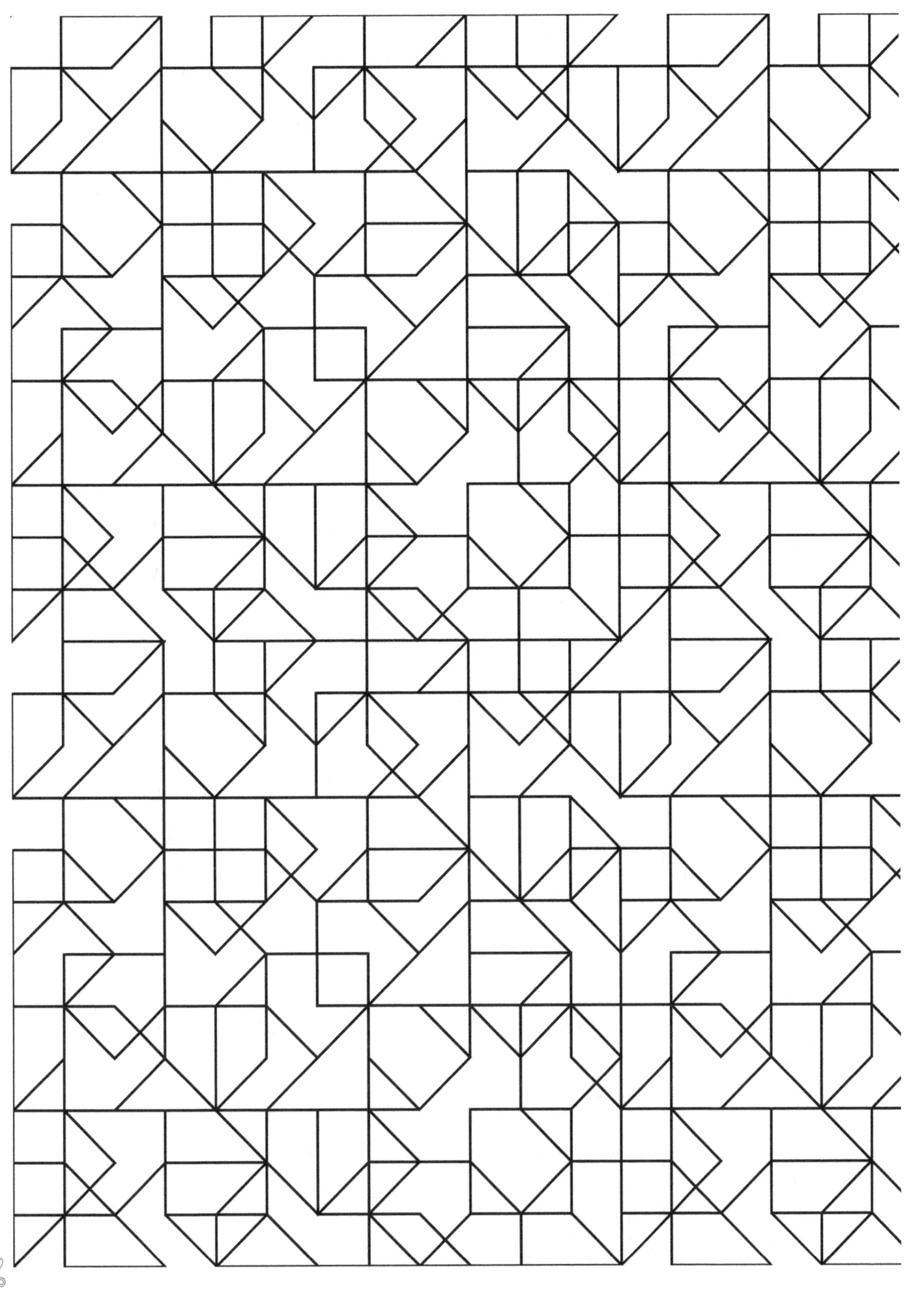

As a Father, I willingly nurture & protect the Soul's of all those I love.

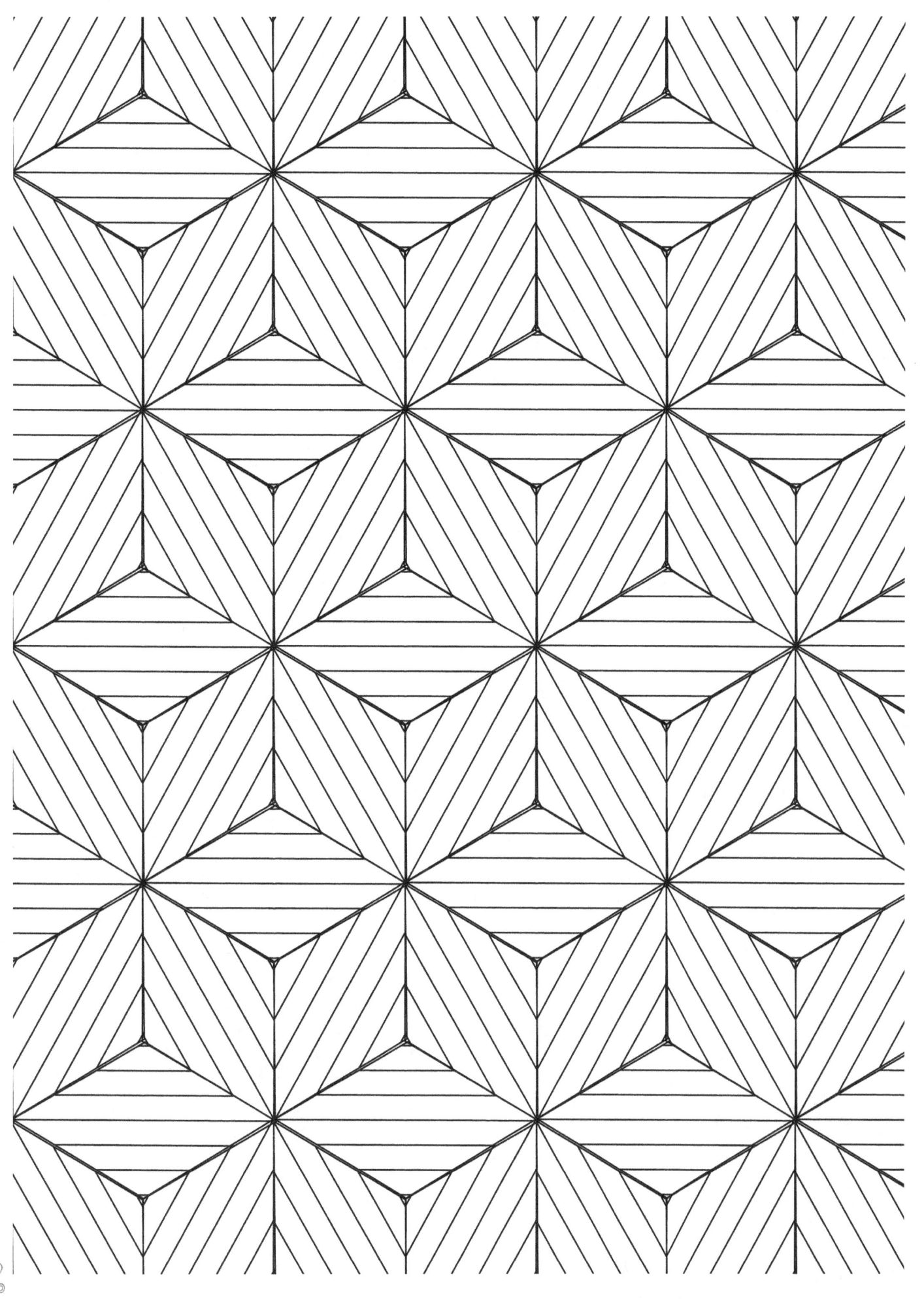